café life
VENICE

A Guidebook to the Cafés and Bacari
of La Serenissima

Written by Joe Wolff
Photography by Roger Paperno

INTERLINK BOOKS

First published in 2009 by

INTERLINK BOOKS

An imprint of Interlink Publishing Group, Inc.
46 Crosby Street, Northampton, Massachusetts 01060
www.interlinkbooks.com

Text copyright © Joe Wolff 2008
Photography copyright © Roger Paperno 2008
Design copyright © Interlink Publishing 2008

Library of Congress Cataloging-in-Publication Data
Wolff, Joe.
Cafe life Venice : a guidebook to the cafes and bacari of La Serenissima / by Joe Wolff ; photography by Joe Paperno.
p. cm. —(Cafe life series)
ISBN 978-1-56656-718-3 (pbk.)
1. Coffeehouses—Italy—Venice—Guidebooks. 2. Bars (Drinking establishments)—Italy—Venice—Guidebooks.
3. Venice (Italy)—Social life and customs. I. Title.
TX907.5.I82V46 2008   647.9545'311—dc22   2008000588

Printed and bound in Korea

To request our 40-page full-color catalog, please visit our website at: www.interlinkbooks.com, call us toll-free at:
1-800-238-LINK, or write to us at: Interlink Publishing, 46 Crosby Street, Northampton, MA 01060
e-mail: info@interlinkbooks.com

Dedicated to Robin, who likes to sit in the sun and drink prosecco.
—JW

To my mother, who always encouraged my dreams.
—RP

CONTENTS

CAFÉ LOCATIONS

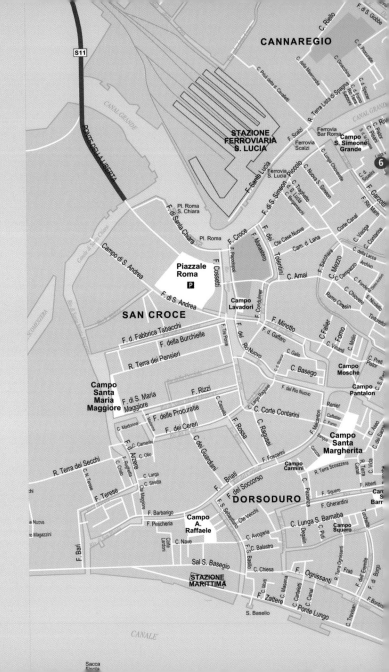

INTRODUCTION

*T*he Café Life series takes you to its third Italian city—*La Serenissima* (the most serene republic)—with *Café Life Venice*. Like predecessors *Café Life Rome* and *Café Life Florence*, it explores a select group of family-run establishments. But because Venice moves to the stroke of its very own gondola paddle (*remo*), you'll be drinking less coffee, eating less gelato—and sipping more wine. This may be good news to some of you. The Venetians do love their wine, and you'll see them loving it at almost any time of day in one of the city's many *bacari*. The *bacaro* is a cross between a café and a wine bar, where you'll find locals knocking back an *ombra* (Venetian for glass of wine) and eating *cichetti* (tapas-like snacks) as they stand at the bar. The wine that they quaff like water is usually fairly low in alcohol content—around 11 percent.

Bacari are a hidden treasure for a couple reasons: they offer an option to the overpriced, bad food that is so easy to find in Venice, and they help preserve the slowly fading traditional Venetian cuisine. In addition to the bacaro (also called *osteria* or *enoteca*), we've included some superb *pasticcerie* (bakeries), a café or two, and one gelateria. Only one because, unlike Rome and Florence, Venice is not rich in *gelato artigianale* (homemade ice cream). Never mind—drink the wine instead.

Most of these places are, relatively speaking, a good value for the money (remember, Italy is expensive), and run by proprietors obsessed with quality. To bring them to life, we interviewed the owners, got their personal stories, and then photographed them and their neighborhoods. We carefully chose a mixture of establishments sprinkled throughout the *sestieri* of Venice to help you refuel during your wanderings or when you get lost. And count on one thing while in Venice— you *will* get lost. Of course, you can't get seriously lost because Venice isn't that big.

The best time to go is in the winter, when the overwhelming waves of tourists subside. The colder and foggier, the better. Bundle up in your magnificent new Italian wool coat and wander the canals of Cannaregio, between Strada Nuova and Fondamenta Nove. Little has changed in 500 years. It's magic.

La Serenissima can be *difficilissima*; however, *Café Life Venice* will help make it *piacevole* (pleasurable).

We want to thank JoAnn Locktov, Ivo Neri, Giorgio Zoccoletto, and Paulo Juris. Without their invaluable help, suggestions, and connections, this book would not have been written. And many thanks to our agent Julie Hill, the force behind making the Café Life series a reality, plus a *mille grazie* to our copyeditor, Elise O'Keefe, and our Italian proofreader, Costanzo Buzzelli. Joe would especially like to thank his wife, Robin, for her love and support.

Also, many thanks to the charming and comfortable Ca' Gottardi Hotel in Cannaregio (www.cagottardi.com). Our hosts—Tatiana, her brother, Gabriele, and her father, Vittorio—made our stay in Venice *molto comodo*.

And of course, our gratitude to all the fiercely proud Venetians we interviewed for this book. The following sums up their feelings about La Serenissima: Why did the Venetians build a bridge to *terra ferma* (the mainland)? So the rest of Europe wouldn't feel like an island.

CANNAREGIO

Cannaregio encompasses a piece of Venice stretching from the train station down almost to the Rialto Bridge. They say the name is either a corruption of canal regio *(royal canal), or that it comes from the* canne *(reeds) that once grew there. The 20,000 inhabitants make it the second largest of Venice's six* sestieri *(districts). Away from the main artery Strada Nuova, you'll discover much of this traditionally working-class area can be* tranquillo.

Alla Vedova

Ramo Ca' d'Oro
Cannaregio 3912
041 5285324
Open 11:30AM–2:30PM, 6:30–10:30PM,
Monday to Wednesday, Friday & Saturday
6:30–11PM, Sunday
Closed Thursdays
Closed during August

*I*n Venice, a *ramo* is a very short street—like Ramo Ca' d'Oro, which hits Calle del Pistor right outside the front door of Alla Vedova. This traditional bacaro's real name is Ca' d'Oro, but no one calls it that.

In the 1890s, owner Renzo's great-grandfather came from Brindisi to sell the region's strong wine, like many other Pugliesi, and eventually opened a bacaro (see the All'Arco entry for more on the Pugliesi in Venice). The bacaro passed on to Renzo's grandfather and grandmother, who ran it for many years—and then something strange happened. His grandfather, Enrico, sold the bacaro to a young man named Mario. During the *compravendita* (sale), Mario fell in love with Enrico's daughter, Rachele. The young couple (soon to be Renzo's parents) married and the bacaro ended up staying in the family. Unfortunately, Mario died young in 1963, and his *vedova* (widow) ran the place alone for another 40 years. The locals would say, *"Andiamoa a bere un bicchiere dalla vedova"* (Let's go have a glass of wine at the widow's place). And so, the name remained.

Renzo studied medicine for three years before, as he says, "I got fed up and came to work here. I've been here since 1976." His sister, Mirella, runs the place with him.

In his deep melodious voice (he should be doing voice-over work), he'll tell you, "I'm a man who thinks about a lot of things, *ma poi fa ben poco* (but then does little). I have to start some things."

Of course, this is not exactly true. He's a *collezionista*—that is to say, when he is not working, he collects things. "I have 27 cameras," he continues. "Some from the '60s and two or three that are very rare. I began collecting ten years ago, and then it became a mania. You buy catalogs and you

see things, and then you want them. I also started a photographic library. I now have about 100 books."

Renzo is partial to photographers who capture "everyman" going about his daily business. "I like the portraits of the street," he says. At the top of his list sits Robert Doisneau (1912–1994), the Frenchman who specialized in shooting the common folk of Paris.

Another favorite, Brassai, born Jules Halasz in Brasov, Hungary (1899–1984), came to Paris as a journalist in 1918 and began working with the camera. Nicknamed the "Eye of Paris" by writer Henry Miller, he spent most of his life photographing the flow of humanity in his adopted city.

Renzo also likes the high-profile Henri Cartier-Bresson (1908–2004), but not as much as he likes Doisneau and Brassaï. Considered the father of modern photojournalism and a master of candid photography, Cartier-Bresson remained a devotee of the 35-mm camera during his entire career.

Renzo's second hobby is collecting classic Italian model trains. And he has a plan that combines both of his hobbies—a trip across the United States by train while he does a little photography. "A month or two with the right companion, maybe a *bella ragazza*. It's difficult to find the right companion," he says.

A lifelong resident of Venice, Renzo loves his city. But he admits it can provide an insular existence. He explains, "The risk is you forget life outside, and this becomes a very small world. There is an advantage because you're protected, but the danger is that you think, 'If it's okay here, it's okay in the rest of the world.' And this is not true. Outside there is a world that changes."

Which is not to say Venice hasn't changed. Although it has always been a tourist city, there was a period—even 20 years ago—when few visitors arrived in winter. Tourism began in the spring and ended at the Regata Storica (a big race on the Grand Canal), on the first Sunday in September. Now, it's nonstop tourists—roughly 12 million a year.

"When I was growing up in the 1950s, Venice was a lot different," says Renzo. "Much simpler and much poorer. This is one of the problems with Italians. They have forgotten what it was like to be poor, to think of things in a simpler way. It would be great if we could combine simplicity with having money. We're in a period of spiritual crises because in the '70s, '80s, '90s there was a lot of money around."

Italy is also experiencing another type of crisis. The country's post-World War II economic miracle—*il sorpasso*—peaked in 1987, when Italy's gross domestic product (GDP) exceeded that of the United Kingdom. It stayed competitive by continual devaluation of the lira, but then with the advent of the euro, this strategy

was no longer possible. Italy had to live with the fixed single European currency and the cost of living has risen dramatically, while the quality of life has suffered.

One positive thing about the Venetian spirit is the continued use of dialect, points out Renzo. Even today it is commonly spoken by poor, middle class, and rich alike—an unpretentious means of communication and leveler of society.

The Venetian dialect is as unpretentious as Renzo's menu, which he describes as *tipico* and *semplice*. Sit at a table and order pasta with clams or shrimp, or a lasagna with radicchio and sausage, or the spring special *pastisso de asparagi* (pasta with asparagus). You can also stand and snack on classic *cichetti* (snacks) at the aging marble-topped counter: *baccalà mantecato* (salt cod on toast), great *polpette* (meatballs), fried artichokes, *seppie arrostite* (grilled cuttlefish), and octopus. When the barista asks what you want to drink with your *cichetti*, don't say, "Water." Because he'll say, "If you want water, go out to the canal." You want to order the appropriate *ombra* (glass of wine).

As for the next generation at Alla Vedova, it's an uncertainty. Renzo has two sons, 18-year-old twins. In his smooth, easy-listening voice, he explains, "They're going to the university, but they say, 'Don't sell the osteria. It's possible we might want to work here.' They know there's a problem finding work after you graduate."

You can tell he is very proud of his boys.

Calle del Pistor, one of the streets that defines the corner where you'll find this bacaro, takes its name from pistori, *an old Venetian word for baker. This street was the location of bread shops or small bakeries. Historically, two-thirds of the population worked in the various trades, and you'll notice other streets named for them:* Frezzerie *(arrow makers),* Botteri *(barrel makers),* Fabbri *(blacksmiths),* Saonieri *(soap makers),* Spadieri *(sword makers),* Tintori *(cloth dyers),* Calegheri *(makers of gondolier shoes), and* Luganegheri *(sausage makers). Of course, all of this is very interesting, but you're really here for the excellent cichetti and a glass of wine or two.*

Pasticceria Ballarin

Salizada San Giovanni Grisostomo
Cannaregio 5794
O41 5285273
Open daily 7:30AM–8PM

As you ramble down the *strada principale*—the main drag that changes names frequently—on the way to the Rialto, you might pass right by Pasticceria Ballarin. This would be a mistake.

It's a cheery, stand-at-the-counter bar/pasticceria run by the Ballarin brothers. Behind the bar you have Luca, the handsome one, and Diego, the industrious, smiling one. Andrea and Michele, the ones who make all of the wonderful pastries, labor around the corner in a cramped *laboratorio* (workshop).

It takes ten employees, from shop assistants to pastry makers, to run the place, which is open every day of the year. "We don't focus on the tourists," says Andrea. "They come here, which is good, but we really work to make the Venetians happy. Sunday is a big day. They buy lots of pastries. Also around Carnevale. We make 90 percent of what we sell."

Pastry makers for about fifteen years, Andrea and Michele learned their trade in various junior positions. The field continually evolves, and, in order to stay current with the latest machinery and *materie prime* (raw materials), they attend a yearly trade show in Rimini and a biannual one in Verona. Andrea claims the job is like having an *amante* (lover): you need to commit yourself and make sacrifices. Most days, he begins work at 5AM.

When he does take time off, he likes to travel and has visited France, Austria, Brazil, Cuba, and the north of England. He says, "I'm very curious to see how other people live. I always learn something."

Andrea and Michele's pastries are superb—in the biscotti department: crunchy (and ubiquitous) *pan del doge*, orange-flavored *baicoli* (little jokes in Venetian), *zaletti* made with cornmeal and lemon peel or raisins, and sweet S-shaped *busolai* with slight anisette flavor. In the not-to-be-missed, words-will-fail-you department, you have both the *certosino al cioccolato*—which looks like a heavy chocolate-covered fruit cake, but is instead light and slightly nougaty with bits of candied fruit—and the *rondelle d'arancio*, candied Sicilian orange slices dipped in the finest dark chocolate.

And, of course, anything filled with Andrea and Michele's *crema* (custardlike pastry cream) is exceptional. "Our strong point is our crema," Andrea explains. "It's not too strong, not too aromatic, but with a consistent flavor. We use only pure, unsweetened cream. When we took this place over in 2000, we decided to push the quality—substituting butter for margarine, natural flavoring for artificial, fresh eggs instead of eggs in a box, Italian almonds, and real vanilla, not synthetic. We use chocolate with a minimum of 72 percent cocoa.

"You can talk to people about the difference in taste between 70, 50, or 22 percent cocoa, but they don't understand until they taste the chocolate. It's the same with the orange slices from Sicily."

Ballarin profits from lots of foot traffic. You'll notice the bustle when you stop in for your morning brioche and cappuccino. It's not just the pastry that draws the crowds—the pasticceria also serves excellent coffee, in a city that, ironically, is less than a mecca for good coffee (even though its first coffeehouse opened in 1683).

You may have wondered about the origin of San Giovanni Grisostomo, the namesake for Ballarin's street or *salizada*. Also called John Chrysostom, this saint served as a Christian bishop of Constantinople from late 398 to early 403. His Greek surname/nickname *chrysosotomos* (golden-mouthed) was bestowed on him because of his eloquence in public speaking.

St. John's homilies emphasized the spiritual and temporal needs of the poor and spoke out against abuses of wealth and power. As bishop of Constantinople, he had many privileges, including the right to host lavish banquets. He refused all of this worldliness, which put him in good with the common man and in not so good with the clergy, the rich, and the emperor.

An extreme ascetic, St. John became a hermit in his mid-twenties and spent two sleep-deprived years learning the Bible by heart—while standing. As you can imagine, this did not do wonders for his health; consequently, he suffered permanent stomach and kidney damage.

Eventually, St. John's enemies formed an alliance and had him banished; a few years later, he died in exile. He is now, however, honored as a saint by the Roman Catholic Church, Eastern Catholic Church, and the Orthodox Church.

Some controversy surrounds St. John Chrysostom's anti-Jewish homilies, which were used by Nazi spin doctors to justify the Holocaust. At the end of World War II, both Christian scholars and the Catholic Church denounced this approach, explaining that Chrysostom's remarks must be taken in historical context—the late 300s were a time when the Christian church was struggling to survive, and the rhetorical style of the day was to slam any opposing view aggressively.

The "salizada" of Salizada San Giovanni Grisostomo refers to a street that was originally dirt or grass and often very wide. The *salizadas* were usually the first Venetian streets to be paved. People rode their horses on the *salizadas* until the 1300 or 1400s, when the city fathers decided that the Venetian lifestyle did not really lend itself to horseback.

Your peregrinations down Salizada San Giovanni Grisostomo will take you to the Campo San Bartolomeo and the Rialto Bridge. Just before the bridge, on your right, you'll see a big *palazzo* (building), the Fondaco dei Tedeschi. First built in 1228, it served as offices for accountants and other bean-counter types who oversaw the commercial activities of the Rialto area. Eventually, the Venetians decided trade with German merchants was so

important that they set aside this structure as a combined warehouse, living area, and trading center for them—Fondaco dei Tedeschi. *Fondaco*, from the Arabic *fondouk*, means "warehouse" or "depot," and *Tedeschi* means "Germans," though the Venetians used it as an umbrella term to include Austrians, Hungarians, and Northern Europeans in general. This was the original work/live space.

The Fondaco dei Persiani stood right next door, and other important foreign trading partners had depots in the city, such as Fondaco dei Turchi and Campo dei Mori.

Generally, Venetians were very tolerant of foreigners, as conveyed in this passage by Lady Anna Miller describing the crowded Piazza San Marco in her *Letters from Italy...in the Years 1770 and 1771*:

Here are the senators, nobles, merchants, fine ladies, and the meanest of people: Jews, Turks, puppets, Greeks, mountebanks, all sorts of jugglers and sights. Although such a heterogeneous mixture of people throng the place during the day, and often pass a great part of the night here, yet there is no riot or disturbance: the Venetians are so accustomed to see strangers, as not to be the least surprised at their being dressed in a fashion different from themselves; nor inclined to esteem them objects of ridicule, on account of their not speaking the Venetian language…

The initial Fondaco dei Tedeschi burned down and the present edifice was built between 1506 and 1508—larger than the original, with five stories and more than 200 rooms. Inside, a gallery on each floor looks down at the open courtyard and fountain (though that was covered over in 1937). Frescoes by Titian and Giorgione adorned the exterior.

The building's design allowed its Venetian custodian to track who came and went (making sure no *prostitute* or *delinquenti* entered), and also to keep an eye on the Tedeschi's flow of money and arms. (Spying was a major government pastime in Venice.) Napoleon booted out the Tedeschi in 1806 and turned the Fondaco into a customs house. It was recycled once again in 1870 to become Venice's central post office.

Drop by Ballarin first thing in the morning for your cappuccino. You may also feel the urge to sample one of the luscious pastries on display——everything made with the best ingredients. Don't miss the certosino al cioccolato—*it looks like fruitcake, but it's light, nougaty, and drizzled in dark chocolate. Come back later, at aperitivo time, for a* spritz *(white wine, Campari, twist of lemon peel, shot of seltzer). You'll rub elbows with well-dressed Venetians, and possibly the resident pigeon with a sweet tooth that pops in numerous times during the day and wanders around the floor cleaning up the crumbs.*

La Cantina

Strada Nuova, Campo San Felice
Cannaregio 3689
041 5228258
Open 10AM–10PM
Closed Sundays
Closed two weeks July to August & two weeks in January

The two owners of La Cantina, Francesco Zorzetto and Andrea Zanatta, are very cool guys. Not only do both of their last names begin with the letter "Z," but they have managed to create an unpretentious bacaro/enoteca that attracts Venetians and tourists like flies to honey.

Andrea, the charming one behind the bar, does his best to offer something from his excellent selection of wines. Chef Francesco, with a sense of humor as dry as a glass of Verdicchio, works from the raised, open cooking area to the side of the bar, where he creates various *piatti* (dishes)—an artist who paints culinary landscapes for your palate.

Andrea and Francesco met when they were seven years old, and grew up almost next door to each other in Martellago, a town about 20 kilometers northwest of Venice. They played together and attended the same schools, until they got older when Andrea enrolled in an *istituto technico* to study electronics and Francesco went to a *scuola alberghiera* (culinary and hotel school).

"I went to a hotel school, but I didn't study," says Francesco. "I got a diploma, but I wasn't committed or dedicated. It was a disaster. I learned to cook after I got

out. When you get out of one of these schools, there's no big problem getting a job because in that field there's always a need for people. You always find a place."

"I had a great ambition to work for myself," he continues. "I didn't want to be a *dipendente* (employee). Four years after I finished school, I had my own place. I was only 23."

Meanwhile, Andrea worked as an electrician during the week and as a waiter or barista on weekends for a little extra cash—and because he liked the food business.

"In 1994, Francesco got a bar in Venice and asked me if I wanted to be his partner. I said yes. And we started on this adventure. I figured if it didn't work, I'd go back to being an electrician," explains Andrea.

After three years as partners in their first venture, they had problems renewing the license and had to close. "We were out on the street, so to speak," says Andrea. Then they heard that the present location was for rent. It had been a combination bar/sweet shop, selling *biscotti* (cookies), *cioccolatini* (chocolates), and *caramelle* (caramels). Before that it was a small grocery store and also a *drogheria* or dry goods store that sold things like detergents, canned goods, spices, and wine. "We were more interested in the bar because we had experience in that area. The chocolates and caramels were not exactly our thing," explains Andrea. "When the former clientele were used to the fact that we added breakfast and panini to the bar, we got up our courage, about eight months after we opened, and eliminated the sweets."

At first they served panini with prosciutto crudo, mozzarella, and asiago (a local cheese), then expanded to include *crostini*, which are thin slices of lightly toasted bread, usually topped with a variety of spreadable paté-type goodies. From there, the menu continued evolving along with Francesco's skill as a chef. He created dishes that were as *belli* as they were tasty. And he began to experiment with seafood because fresh fish is readily available at the nearby *pescheria* (Venice fish market). Soon they were selling more fish than *salumi e formaggi* (cold meats, salami, and cheese). Says Andrea, "Our fish menu is unpredictable. It depends on what is available fresh from market. If the fish isn't fresh, we don't buy it. And if there is nothing good fresh, then we don't serve fish."

It is this spontaneity that separates La Cantina from the traditional bacaro where everything is prepared ahead of time and presented in a glass display case on the counter. "We'd rather make everything fresh while you wait. People wait a little more, but a dish that's made to order is much healthier," adds Andrea." People who know us don't mind waiting for one of Francesco's creations. The menu comes from Francesco's imagination. He's free to do what he wants."

Francesco's philosophy about creativity and cooking guides him in developing La Cantina's menu. To begin with, there is no specialty of the house. "A cook that has a specialty is limited," says Francesco. "He uses the same recipes. I don't like the idea of people coming here to eat our typical dishes. When you eat the *tipici*, you often eat things that are not good. A cook has to create, and not serve up food like it's coming from a factory. You should go for the cook and what he wants to create, and his spirit."

As a chef, Francesco feels that he has creative cycles. "It's like being a writer," he says. "Sometimes you want to write and sometimes you don't want to write. But you have to do it anyway." And, like many artists, Francesco rides the roller coaster of depression. "I suffer a lot from depression," he adds. "And when I do, I don't have a desire to create."

In that case, what does he do? He makes his food from memory, not passion. There is a subtle difference in taste that only he can notice. For everyone else, whether the emotional roller coaster goes up or down, the food Francesco prepares is always marvelous. You'll sample his crostini—*canocchia* (a small crustacean) and onion sauce, *tonno crudo con asparagi* (raw tuna with asparagus), tongue with fresh horseradish shavings, salted beef with smoked ricotta and chopped pickle. Or maybe try some of his other dishes, such as sea bass with *fagiolini* (small tender string beans), *polpi con sedano biancho* (octopus with white celery), *pesce spada scottato in salsa di curry e sesame nero* (swordfish charred in a sauce of curry and black sesame), and *rombo crudo* (turbot) drizzled with a mixture of olive oil, lemon, and salt.

Along with his creative freedom, Francesco greatly values his partnership and friendship with Andrea: "Andrea is a great person. If it wasn't for him I couldn't go on."

At the bar, Andrea greets you with his sincere smile. Wine is his specialty. In the early days, they had only two or three types. Since then, he has expanded La Cantina's selection to include vintages from the north and south of Italy as well as

from Spain and France. Knowledge-able about wine (and self taught), he says humbly, "Every day, I learn something."

As with the kitchen, there is no *specialità della casa*—it's what you prefer, and for those who aren't sure, Andrea will advise. "If you like *vino aromatico*, we try to offer a choice between a Gewürztraminer and a sauvignon, or for those that like younger wines, it's a Valpolicella. Then again, maybe you like a heavier Barbera, Chianti, or Sicilian red."

Besides knowing his wine, Andrea is an accomplished fine arts photographer, whose work is featured in local shows and in his book, *Andrea Zanatta Venezia*.

So, who comes in to La Cantina? It's about a 50/50 mix of locals and tourists. You might sip a glass of Amarone next to an Italian visiting from Palermo or a barrel-chested, middle-aged Venetian who looks like a *gondoliere*. The latter being the case, you're probably standing beside Vittorio Costantini, a La Cantina neighbor. He looks like a gondoliere because he was one for 37 years, until he retired and opened nearby Ca' Gottardi Hotel with son Gabriele and daughter Tatiana, just up the Strada Nuova from Andrea and Francesco, on the small canal called Rio di Noale. "Instead of hosting people in my gondola, I now host them in my hotel," says Vittorio. The Costantini family renovated a 15th-century palazzo that stood empty for 30 years to create their comfortable and elegant hotel, a nice mix of traditional Venetian and contemporary style.

You could also be standing next to actress Juliette Binoche of *Chocolat* (2000) and *The English Patient* (1996) fame, who has come in four or five times as a customer—and once as an actress. She starred in the spy drama *A Few Days in September* (2006), which used La Cantina as a location. The film's Argentinean director, Santiago Amigorena, rented the place for a day in October 1995 to shoot a scene at the bar.

Australian director Roger Donaldson also favors La Cantina—he stops in whenever he and his wife are in town, and sends a Christmas card every year. Donaldson's credits include *The Bounty* (1984), *No Way Out* (1987), *Thirteen Days* (2000), and *The World's Fastest Indian* (2005).

Venetian resident and film composer Pino Donaggio is another regular. Born on the island of Burano, he made his soundtrack debut with a score for the classic thriller set in Venice entitled *Don't Look Now* (1973), and eventually moved to Hollywood where he collaborated regularly with Brian De Palma. Since the mid–1980s, Donaggio has made Italy the focus of his work.

And for fans of the ABC Emmy-winning castaways drama *Lost*, and in particular of actor Matthew Fox, who plays Dr. Jack Shepherd, you may have the opportunity to be served a glass of wine by Matthew's sister-in-law Giulia, an employee at La Cantina. Matthew met Giulia's sister Margherita, a former model, in New York City between his sophomore and junior year at Columbia University. The chemistry

between the two was like a *colpo di fulmine* (bolt of lightening). Word must have gotten out that Matthew married a local girl because you see autographed pictures of the actor in the windows of a few small businesses around the city.

Informale e molto relax—those are the houses rules, says Andrea. "You can start with a small taste of fish and then maybe have some cheese. It all depends on how hungry you are. We're very flexible."

Sit inside or "hang" at one of La Cantina's outside tables and watch Venice cruise by as you drink wine. In fact, why not make this corner of Cannaregio your neighborhood. There's a Billa grocery store almost across the street. Buy a Tim Card for your mobile phone at the office supply a few doors down. Extract euros from a convenient ATM. Sleep at nearby Ca' Gottardi Hotel (www.cagottardi.com). Life is good.

Torrefazione Caffé Costarica

Rio Terrà San Leonardo
Cannaregio 1337
O41 716371
Open 8AM–1PM, 2:30PM–5:30PM
Closed Sundays, except in December

Normally, you smell Torrefazione Caffé Costarica before you see it. The seductive aroma of roasting coffee beans grabs you by the olfactory lobes and pulls you in the door. It's like the old days when there were many small coffee-roasting establishments such as this, and the owners would pipe the fabulous smell through vents under the door or windows in order to draw people inside. Now, Costarica is the last one of its kind—the only *torrefazione* (roasting house) left in Venice.

Once inside, you'll see—behind the 75-kilo bags of coffee beans and the old wooden counter—a roasting machine that looks like it came from an H. G. Wells tale. For years it was operated by the wiry 70-something proprietor, Camillo Marchi. Unfortunately, Camillo passed away in December 2006, during the writing of this book. His family continues to run the business; this chapter is dedicated to him.

Camillo's grandmother, Antonia Modolo, opened the business in 1930. A woman with a stern demeanor, she came from Udine in Friuli, where they had a reputation for being *grande lavaratori* (hard workers), to join her husband who worked at the port. She chose coffee roasting because her son imported coffee beans.

"My grandmother didn't make a *miscela* (blend) like I do. It wasn't great. Because you have to understand that the *vecchi Veneziani* (old Venetians) used to cook *chicchi crudi* (raw beans) in *una palla di caffé* (an iron ball) over a gas flame. It was a bit primitive," said Camillo, who would gladly have shown you the palla if you'd asked him. The business passed from his grandmother to his mother, Emilia, and then to him, and it has been open continuously except for a few years during World War II.

Camillo learned how to blend coffee by doing it and became a true artist with the beans. His recipe is a secret, which he adjusted yearly according to the weather. Every year the coffee changes, like the grapes.

"When I smell the raw beans, I understand," he explained. "I see and I smell what flavor is inside before I roast. When I prepare a blend, I know how it is going to taste in the cup. I remove a little of this, add a little of that. It has to have a sweet flavor and not upset your stomach. I use the highest-quality arabica, which is not hard on the liver, with naturally lower caffeine. It is the robusto that upsets your stomach."

To help you "talk coffee" when the need arises, here is a little primer on arabica and robusto.

Coffea arabica is the species name for the original coffee plant, discovered in Ethiopia, where it still grows wild. The plant likes high altitudes, volcanic-type soil, and warm climates. Usually, the better arabica is grown at altitudes of 3,000 to 4,500 feet and referred to as "hard bean." Above 4,500 feet, when things get really serious, it's called "strictly hard bean." Generally, the harder the arabica bean the more flavorful the coffee. Arabica beans are used in the best coffees.

Coffea robusta, on the other hand, has become the bean of choice for big commercial coffee producers because it offers more resistance to disease and the ability to grow at lower altitudes, where there's more rain and higher temperatures. The Congo, Cameroon, and Angola produce robusto. With this bean, you sacrifice the aroma and flavor found in arabica. The cheaper robusto beans contain as much as 40 percent more caffeine than better-quality arabica.

The longer the roast, the darker the coffee—and darker means less caffeine (as much as 15 percent less) because it's burned up in the roasting process. This information should clear the name of the poor dark espresso bean, which has gotten a bad rap all these years for being high in caffeine content.

Almost every day, Camillo created his *miscela* and roasted it in his 1961 vintage *tostatrice* (roasting machine) from Bologna. The tostatrice holds four kilos at a time, which Camillo took from the 75-kilo coffee sacks piled inside the door. Using a *sgozzadone,* the unfortunate name for a small spade ("sgozzadone" literally means "to slit a woman's throat"), he extracted a dribble of beans in his *sesola* (Venetian for scoop).

Roasting the four kilos took about 40 minutes, and afterwards, he left the machine idling so it could pull air through the beans and cool them. New deliveries still arrive every three days. Only the best for Caffé Costarica—you'll see sacks marked with the names Terrazu, a superb Costa Rican coffee; Colum Especial, a high-grade Columbian; and Guatemalan Genuine Antigua, considered one of the world's great beans.

Although neither of his two children followed him into the business, he was very proud of what they have accomplished, and he was careful to explain that they did it "without the help of their papa." His son runs his own law firm with two offices and his daughter owns a public relations firm in Milano, employing 15 people.

Camillo said, "I'm of the opinion that if you can't do a job well, it's better not to do it. You're not going to be successful. In Venice, around 40 years ago, there were 20 *torrefazioni di caffé.* When the supermarkets arrived, these people wanted to compete, so they bought cheaper inferior beans. I continued to buy the best. They're all closed, and we're still here."

People from all over Europe come to Caffé Costarica—its special blend of *Caffé della Sposa* (Bride's Coffee) makes them happy. The following is the story behind the name, written by Camillo:

> The wedding day arrived for a splendid young Venetian woman, and that morning, after she dressed in white, she felt faint with emotion. Her mother said, "Nothing to fear, yesterday I visited Camillo, the *tostatore* (coffee roaster) of Venice. He knew

you were getting married and gave me this blend of coffee that he made especially for you. It's blended so that when you drink it, you'll feel the strength to help you experience a day you'll never forget." The bride grew strong from the coffee, and the coffee grew sweet from the bride. For this reason, it's called *Caffé della Sposa*.

Caffé della Sposa is blended with the finest arabica beans from Costa Rica, Columbia, Guatemala, Brazil, Haiti, India, Ethiopia, and San Salvador. This brew has attracted strange bedfellows, such as world-famous diva Maria Callas, and Greg Perry, author of the high-tech, self-help bible *C Programming in 12 Easy Lessons*, whose book is inscribed, "Thank you to Camillo e Loredana Marchi, who made me feel at home here in Venice. Your caffé Costarica is the best in the world. This book is for you."

Caffè Costarica sits on Rio Terrà San Leonardo, a street bordering the Ghetto (a Venetian gift to the world's vocabulary). The term comes from the word *gettare* (to smelt) and the Venetian word for foundry—*geto*.

In the 1300s and 1400s, a small island in Cannaregio was the site of the first Venetian foundries; eventually (after the foundries moved to the Arsenale), it became the place where the Jews were confined.

Jews lived and traded in Venice without "official sanction" until 1385, when they received the right to reside there, practice usury, and sell used clothing. Then, in 1397, they were expelled, but still allowed to stay in Venice for 15 consecutive days at a time. The ostensible reason for this was Jewish banking irregularities, but the real reason was the fear they would infiltrate other areas of business and gain too much economic power. Everyone followed this 15-day rule, sort of, for another hundred years.

As part of the deal, Jews had to distinguish themselves from Christians by wearing, initially, a piece of yellow cloth (1394), then later, a yellow skull cap (1496), and finally, in 1500, a red hat. Other laws applied only to the Jews, such as the one passed on July 19, 1429, which stated that if a Jewish man was caught "lying with" a Christian woman, he paid a fine of 500 lire and spent six months in prison. For a prostitute, he paid 500 lire and forfeited a year of his life in jail.

Pope Julius II did not like the Venetians—they were too independent minded, and, even worse, they had seized papal territory on the death of his predecessor Pope Alexander VI in 1503. So he formed the League of Cambrai, whose members included France, Spain, Hungary, Mantua, and Ferrara. The League defeated the Venetian army, and then eventually collapsed under its own bickering weight. During this time of upheaval on *terra ferma*, the Jews sought refuge in Venice, which left the Venetians with some mixed feelings. On one hand the republic needed Jewish money; on the other, they did not want large numbers of Jews living among them. Consequently, they took the practical Venetian approach: the Jews could stay, but were segregated in the Ghetto. The year—1516.

It was common practice around the Mediterranean to house foreign merchants in a separate area, however not in such an extreme and isolated manner as with Venice's Jews. They lived in a quarter surrounded by canals and linked to the rest of the city by two bridges that closed from dusk until dawn. In essence, the Jews were locked in at night by armed Christian guards, whose salary they were forced to pay.

At first, about 1,300 people crowded into the small ghetto area, but by the mid-1600s the population had grown to 5,000. As it grew, the only way to expand was upward, with five- to seven-story buildings. Each story had to be as low as possible for the entire structure to provide the most accommodation and still fit within official building parameters—one-third taller than the maximum height for the rest of Venice. And still, there were not enough beds for everyone. And the Jews in Venice did not even own these buildings, because they could not acquire property, and, in addition, they had to pay one third more rent than Christians.

Life centered around the *campi* (squares) lined with shops run by pawnbrokers, usurers, and merchants in the rag trade. During the day, Christians flocked to the Jewish quarter to do business. At night, only Jewish doctors (another sanctioned profession) were allowed to leave the Ghetto to visit patients.

The Venetians quite happily kept the Jews as moneylenders because they could be easily controlled and heavily taxed. As Shakespeare put it in *The Merchant of Venice*, the Jews were borrowed from—"Let him look to his bond"—and at the same time, spat on—"You call me misbeliever, cut-throat dog. And spet upon my Jewish gaberdine."

The Jews stayed segregated in the Ghetto until 1797, when Napoleon demolished its gates during the French occupation.

After touring the Ghetto, come by Caffé Costarica for a cappuccino. When Camillo was there, if you spoke Italian, you could have asked him about the soccer match and the *galline padovane*, one of his favorite stories. *Galline padovane* (Paduan chickens) are unique birds with a magnificent glossy coat and a thicket of feathers on their heads that makes them look like they're wearing a fur hat and a beard. Originally Polish, the chickens were brought to Padua from Krakow in the 1300s by the Marchese Giovanni detto Dondi DallOrologio, who became fascinated by their beauty. Some say the ancestry of the *gallina padovana* can also be traced back to a very similar Dutch chicken that wears only the fur hat.

For centuries the gallina padovana has been the gastronomic symbol of Padua. The Padovani take these chickens very seriously and there are strict rules for breeding and eating. Each chicken requires four square meters for free-range feeding (a diet supplemented with maize), a table-ready chicken must be 12 months old and have finished its first egg production cycle, and every bird comes with a *marchio registrato* (registered mark), guaranteeing its origin, much like a bottle of DOC wine.

The *gallo padovano* (rooster) is a symbol of the Padua soccer team, and this is where Camillo's story comes in. "One Sunday, I was a ball retriever for the local soccer game. When there was a game with Padua, the Padavani used to bring *galline padovane*. They'd let them go, and I grabbed one while it was wandering around. And I took it home. If they caught you stealing a chicken, they kicked you out," said Camillo. He loved this story about putting one over on the Padovani, and would laugh infectiously. The rivalry between the cities of Venice and Padua has a long history, and, during most of it, Padua has had an inferiority complex.

Another of Camillo's favorite stories involves the infamous *acqua alta* (high water) that plagues Venice regularly. Under normal circumstances, Camillo put a little dam across the bottom of the door. "I putty the wood and it swells up and blocks the water. We're sailors here in Venezia. We know how to make wood waterproof. A little comes under the wood, and I pump it out. The bags of coffee are up off of the floor about a couple centimeters," he said.

The year 1994 brought higher than normal *acqua alta*. "The water was above the counter. I didn't have a pump then," he explained. "At that point, I used gasolio for heating. And everything was filthy with gasolio and water. A French journalist waded in with all this photography equipment and no wet suit. He stepped on a banana peel and slipped, falling completely under the water. I grabbed him and pulled him up. He was covered in oil and grime."

Make sure you pick a time to visit Caffé Costarica when the *acqua* is not too *alta*, and the coffee beans are roasting—you'll feel like you stepped back 50 years.

Venetians were the first to import coffee beans from Arabia in 1615. Almost 400 years later, Caffé Costarica serves up one of the better coffees in Venice. It's located just before the Ponte delle Guglie on Rio Terrà San Leonardo as you head toward the train station from San Marco. Long ago you would have needed a gondola to traverse Rio Terrà because it was a canal——now filled in with earth.

· 2 ·

SAN MARCO

The heart of the city, and a crowded heart it can be. There's the San Marco sestiere of Piazza San Marco fame, with elbow-to-elbow hordes of two-day trippers. And, believe it or not, there is another part of San Marco, where the Venetians actually live. It is centered on Campo San Anzolo and Campo Santo Stefano, and offers welcome breathing room. Spend some time there.

Bar Aperol

Riva del Ferro
San Marco 5125
041 286304
Open daily 3AM–9PM

*L*et's say you're looking for something to eat in Venice at 3AM. There's only one place to go, because there's only one place open—Bar Aperol. Owner Giorgio Rizzo explains that it's difficult to get a *permesso* (permit) like this in a city known for its early closing times and lack of nightlife. "They gave it to me because the Rialto vaporetto stop is in front of my bar, and the people who live above me didn't protest. And because I'm a *brava persona*—I haven't had any trouble with the *polizia* or *comune*," he adds.

"The only other *permesso* of this type is for the bar inside the fish market on the Isola del Tronchetto. It opens at midnight and closes at 9AM for those people who work there all night. The fish arrive from Padova or Chioggia by truck. Later, the shops and the fish market people go there to buy their product."

When driving to Venice, you cross the bridge from the mainland, Ponte della Libertà, and park your car either at Piazzale Roma or the lot on Tronchetto, an artificial island constructed from landfill during the 1950s with the bad idea of creating a mini-Manhattan.

In 1965, Giorgio began working for his father at Bar Aperol, and, after his dad passed away in 1980, he took over. Although he studied economics for three years at university, he stayed in the family business because he felt it suited him more. A while back, he expanded, forming a partnership with another family to purchase the bars on either side of Aperol.

Giorgio goes to work when you're probably going to bed—midnight. "I work nights because I know the people who come at night, and I know how to handle them. I know almost everyone in Venezia. At night, there are always people a little drunk… you have to stay very alert. Many times I've defused arguments and confrontations. They know when they come here they need to behave. Plus I don't give them a reason to get upset. *Faccio il calmante* (I act like a tranquilizer)." He even studied applied psychology at the local free university, partly to help him hone his people skills.

Years ago, *la gioventù di Venezia* (young people of Venice) gave Giorgio the nickname *mago* (magician). They say, "*Andiamo dal Mago* (Let's go to Mago's)." He earned this name, he explains with great pride, using his very fast hands behind the bar—setting land speed records for making cappuccino and serving tramezzini.

La gioventù often visit Mago on their way home from a late night clubbing on the mainland, especially those from the Lido. They catch the vaporetto at Piazzale Roma, and when it stops in front of Bar Aperol, they hop off, pick up a brioche, *tramezzino*, or *involtino*, and then take a shortcut—about ten minutes on foot—to meet the same lumbering vaporetto at the San Zaccaria stop 20 minutes later.

In addition to quick and tasty food, you'll want to stop here for good coffee (somewhat rare in Venice). Giorgio has served Illy Caffé for a long time. In fact, the company recognized Bar Aperol as Venice's oldest vender of its coffee—since 1966.

"To make a good coffee," he says, "you need a good blend, and you have to maintain your coffee machine, just like a car. It has to be cleaned regularly, you have to check the filters, and make sure you have a certain pressure. And then when it comes to coffee itself—*piu ne fai, piu buoni diventano* (the more you make, the better it is). A bar that makes 1,000 coffees a day will have better coffee than one that makes 50 or 100."

The moment of truth: a rich creamy head or *crema* that makes the perfect espresso. Giorgio says, "When I see an American film, the people always drink coffee from a big pot. The question is how do you like your coffee? *Come stimolante o come bibita* (as a stimulant or a drink)?"

Giorgio has been making coffees for more than 40 years, which makes you wonder: Did he start when he was 5 years old? He looks ten years younger than his age. He's also very well dressed, sporting a dapper fedora, dark glasses, and Allen-Edmonds brogues, the top-of-the-line American shoes—he could be a cast member from *The Sopranos* (but in a good way).

On the morning of November 4, 1966, when the infamous *acqua alta* to end *acqua alta* began to flood Venice, Giorgio was cooking at Bar Aperol. "The water got higher and higher. At 9:30, I went to buy *un paio di stivaloni lunghi* (the long boots that fisherman wear.) They only had three pair in stock because they didn't sell many. We bought two pairs.

"That morning I was walking around Venezia in my big boots. I came to Piazza San Marco and saw a photographer in a motorboat in front of Caffè Florian. So I stood under the portico, watching him. My friend Rico, a gondoliere, came along in a *sandaletto*, which is like a gondola…there was almost 80 centimeters (32 inches) of water in the Piazza."

This was just the beginning—the high tide reached 194 centimeters (76 inches, more than six feet). Although the forecast talked about cloudy skies, choppy seas, and rain, nothing presaged the "perfect storm" that hit the peninsula. Italy stood at the center of two anticyclones or highs. (In the northern hemisphere an anticyclone is a "high" that causes air to circulate in a clockwise direction around its core; the opposite of a cyclone where air rotates in a counterclockwise direction.) Thus, a cold and humid air current from the northwest bumped into a humid current from the east-northeast.

Rain hovered over northeastern Italy causing the Sile, Brenta, and Piave rivers—which run into the Adriatic just north and south of La Serenissima—to overflow their banks, swelling the lagoon. In addition, the dry sirocco blowing off the African continent pushed a huge volume of water north. And if that wasn't enough, there was an abnormally high five-foot tide, which did not have time to flow back out of the lagoon before the next one arrived, due to the excess water from the rains and winds. This produced a double high tide.

The results were catastrophic: Two meter waves hit the ducal palace; a meter and a half of water filled Piazza San Marco; sirocco winds blew at 100 kilometers per hour (60 mph); and there were 25 hours of high tide, with 12 hours of water two meters (six feet) above normal sea level. This added up to Venice's worst-ever flood—the city was cut off for 24 hours. Luckily no one died, unlike the horrific flood that struck Florence at the same time and killed 39 people.

The water rose suddenly, stranding people in bars, restaurants, homes of friends, and in Venice's fourteen movie theaters, which were showing films that included *My Fair Lady*, *Modesty Blaise*, *Genghis Khan*, and *The Sword of Ali Baba*.

Three hundred well-dressed theatergoers at the Teatro del Ridotto saw famed Venetian stage and screen actor Gino Cavalieri in *Il Bugiardo* (*The Liar*), written by equally renowned Venetian playwright Carlo Goldoni, who reformed Italian comedy in the mid-to-late-1700s. After Cavalieri took his bow the audience went to leave, but stopped in their tracks at the top of the stairs leading out of the theater—a half meter of water filled the atrium. No one had boots; there were no *passerelle* (elevated walkways). No one was going anywhere, so management reopened the theater bar and served everyone grappa and brandy.

When the water receded, some Venetians had been stranded in their houses for three days.

In general, Venetians are used to *acqua alta*. It's a seasonal occurrence, and usually, the water rises slowly and descends slowly. (Average high tide is about a foot.) "It doesn't faze us," says Giorgio. "Except for the way it was in 1966."

A siren goes off about three hours before high tide, if it is expected to be 110 centimeters (44 inches) or more, which gives merchants time to move things off the floor and city workers a chance to strategically place *passerelle* around the city. These walkways are about 60 centimeters (24 inches) high, and wide enough for two-way single-file pedestrian traffic. The *Centro maree di Venezia* (Venice Tides Center) also sends out mass text messages to inhabitants' *telefonini* (cell phones) warning of *acqua alta*.

"When the *acqua alta* comes, it's not like a *giorno di riposo* (day off) for us," explains Giorgio. "The water has two cycles—one in the morning and another in the afternoon. In the morning, the water starts to rise around six or seven. We put *passerelle* on the floor in the bar and set the tables on top. Customers eat breakfast with the water right below. They're stable, unless the water gets too high and they start to float. Then, we take them down, and no one can come in the bar for a while."

The customers at Bar Aperol comprise a 60/40 mixture of tourists and locals, and the occasional celebrity, such as Grace Jones. The tall, elegant, Jamaican-born model, singer, and sometimes actress appeared as Zula in *Conan the Destroyer* (1984) and May Day in the James Bond film *A View to a Kill* (also starring Roger Moore and the Golden Gate Bridge).

Whether you're Grace Jones or just a regular person, Giorgio will happily give you directions. Sometimes tourists arrive in the city late, and having stumbled onto Bar Aperol, ask Giorgio how to find their hotel. As with most Venetians, he employs

the *punto di referimento* (point of reference) method. "You can't use addresses," explains Giorgio. "You have to say, 'Take this street, and when you arrive at the end you'll find such and such a store. Go another 200 meters until you see an office supply store, and it's right there.'"

In the early days, the numbers above a Venetian doorway keyed to the personal data of the persons who resided there. Anyone who lived in the house, or moved into the house, used the same number to register a birth, death, or marriage in the state civil registry. Eventually, this proved impractical and the numbers simply became street addresses.

As you wander around Venice, awed by its history, its splendor, and its canals, you might notice a couple of wrinkles—inferior leather products and bad food. Giorgio has an observation on both: "Chinese come here with Chinese mafia money, and invest in businesses. They also set up sweatshops on the mainland with 50 Chinese *clandestini* working day and night. Every so often the Carabinieri come and seize them and send them away. It's true, the wallets and shoes are made in Italy, but the product is not good."

On the other hand, Giorgio knows a woman who bought a good pair of shoes for 100 euros and they gave her problems. So she went to the Chinese vendor near her house and bought a pair for 18. They didn't hurt her feet. She decided that, as an older housewife, living on 800–1000 euros per month, it's easier to buy a cheap coat or pair of shoes, and when they're worn, throw them away. The disposable mentality has slowly crept into Italy.

"The bad food that you find in Venezia is a function of the tourists that come en masse—especially with a tour when the meals are booked ahead of time. The tourist agency works with certain restaurants. They charge you 15–20 euros for mediocre food that costs the restaurant about 8," says Giorgio.

He often ends his day when he gets off work, at about 10:30AM, with a stroll around the city he loves, punctuated by a glass of good wine and *cichetti* at one of his favorite enotecas.

Eccentric, appealing, and efficient, Bar Aperol at the foot of the Rialto Bridge is a good place to stop for a bite at 3 in the morning or 3 in the afternoon. If you're a night owl, you'll meet fellow night owls and owner Giorgio Rizzo. During the day, his son Jeanmanuel works there, along with nine employees. What's to eat? Thirty-six types of tasty tramezzini *(like English tea sandwiches), along with a variety of* involtini *(rolled sandwiches) including* tonno e verdure, mozzarella e olive, *and* provolone e rucola. *Try the excellent coffee, and for your sweet tooth, sample the brioche or* bomboloni *(biscuit-shaped doughnuts filled with jam). You'll mix with gondolieri, businessmen, and tourists.*

Osteria al Bacareto

Calle delle Botteghe
San Marco 3447
041 5289336
Open noon–3PM, 7PM–10:30PM, Monday
to Friday
Noon–3PM, Saturday
Closed Sundays
Closed August

What do running an osteria and training to be a lathe operator have in common? Emilio De Giulio will be the first to tell you: "Nothing." He studied the metalworking trades in school, and he also made keys and worked in his father's heating oil store.

One evening in 1971, Emilio came to buy wine at his local osteria. The owner said he intended to sell the business—would Emilio be interested in buying it? "I was living on a nearby *salizada* (wide street) and came here often. I got along well with the owner," explains Emilio. After thinking it over for only one night, he and his wife Anna said yes. They jumped in, ready for a change, and, as he puts it, "We began this adventure."

Naming it was the easy part—it became Al Bacareto after his grandfather's 1902 osteria. Bacareto is a diminutive of the word *bacaro*, a Pugliese grape vine. Around the turn of the century, many Pugliesi sold their strong, full-bodied wine

(17-percent alcohol) in Venice, and some stayed to open *osterie* and bacari. One theory holds that Venetian bacari take their name from this grape vine. (See the All'Arco entry for more on Pugliese vino in Venice.)

The hard part was getting up to speed on running an osteria. "My experience with food was limited," says Emilio. His sister, Eliana, joined him after a few years. She had small children (as did Emilio and his wife) and family commitments along with a growing business made for some very long days. Plus, there were no employees in this early period.

Although Emilio's sister prepared most of the meals, it was Rosa, a woman in her late 60s who lived nearby and cooked in her own daughter's restaurant, who helped them create Al Bacareto's culinary style. Rosa excelled at *piatti tipici veneziani*

(typical or traditional Venetian dishes), *baccalà*, *seppia*, *bigoli in salsa*. This was 1973.

Full of life and joy and many jokes, Rosa loved the kitchen. "She didn't really get tired at work," says Emilio. "She worked with us five or six years, and then afterwards, often during the day you'd find her at a little table in front of the *locale*. From 10AM until noon she was there holding court—greeting everyone that passed by. She was a type called *comare*." A *comare* is the larger-than-life, middle-aged woman, with an equally big heart, who knows everything that goes on in the neighborhood. An English painter and customer did a portrait of Rosa, which hangs on the wall in the restaurant and captures her joie de vivre.

As they settled in, Emilio's brother-in-law, Meme, joined the business, and the two families moved things forward and made the place the success that it is today. Emilio says, "I believe in a passion for work, but above all a commitment to family is fundamental. With the family as a group behind us, we're able to create a locale that is *buono*."

Emilio functions as the *capo*, although he regards himself more as a point of reference—when a problem arises, employees know there is a manager, someone in authority, to take care of things.

Unfortunately, his sister passed away in 2003. Emilio remembers her fondly as "in the kitchen—*tranquilla*, smiling, always available."

Emilio's wife, Anna, occupies herself with public relations, in addition to keeping an eye on the kitchen and the commissary, and making the sweets. Rather than buy from an industrial bakery or a local pasticceria, she learned to be a pastry maker herself—providing an excellent array of homemade goodies including the ubiquitous tiramisu (her version is special) and a terrific *torta al cioccolata* (chocolate cake).

The oldest of Emilio and Anna's three sons, Adriano, works in the business, as does the youngest Federico, who is still deciding if he'll make the osteria his career. Middle son Alberto has followed a different path—he's an architect. Emilio says,

"I'm proud of all three boys. They're *bravi*. They all have different characteristics. They're disposed to this kind of work because I used to bring them here from the time they were little. They're used to relating to a variety of people, from architects to blue-collar workers."

Both Emilio and Anna come from "the neighborhood." The daughter of a gondoliere, she grew up in the *zona* (area) near Santa Maria del Giglio and he around Santo Stefano. They actually met when they were kids.

Fifty years ago, Venetians found everything inside the small territory of their own zona or *parrocchia* (parish)—unlike the Venice of today where basic services such as shoe repair and dry cleaning are disappearing. There was the *macelleria* (butcher shop), *tostatura di caffé* (coffee roaster), *panetteria* (bread bakery), and even a shop that sold fabric, needles, and thread, plus a myriad of others, including greengrocers, plumbers, carpenters, and artisans.

Al Bacareto draws from *impiegati* (office clerks) and *operai* (blue collar workers and tradesmen) who stand at the bar mornings, to down an *ombra*, snack on *cichetti*, and deliver their opinions on politics and soccer. At lunchtime, the place fills with locals and *pendolari* (commuters), and then, during the evening, the crowd changes to mainly tourists.

The sit-down menu offers a range of classic Venetian dishes that vary daily. Here's what you're likely to find: *spaghetti alle seppie* (pasta in squid ink sauce), *spaghetti alle vongole* (pasta with clams), *bigoli in salsa* (buckwheat pasta with anchovy sauce), *fegato alla Veneziana* (liver with sweet onions), *sardine fritte* (breaded sardines fried in olive oil) and various baccalà dishes—*baccalà mantecato* (salted cod fish on toast, creamed with olive oil), and *baccalà fritto*.

For some, salt-cured and air-dried *baccalà* is an acquired taste; however, most Italians consider it a delicacy. This traditional Baltic cod found its way to Venezia, so the story goes, about 500 years ago when a Venetian trading galley, headed for

England to research new markets, was shipwrecked in a storm on the Norwegian coast. The vessel returned to Venice three years later with a hold full of baccalà. At first not a big hit, the salty fish grew on people, especially sailors when they realized it helped solve the food problem on long voyages. Eventually, the Venetians traded spices for *baccalà*, as it became more in demand by the average Veneziani.

The history of Al Bacareto's building goes back almost as far as Venice's love affair with salty cod. "The *travi* (beams) on the ceiling give you an idea of its age," explains Emilio. "The Brenta and Piave rivers carried tree trunks into the lagoon so they could be transported to Venezia, where they were used in construction. They're marked by an *incisione* (an incision, like a brand). The owner of the trunks and sometimes the eventual destination were identified by the marks carved in each trunk. You can still see this mark on the beam in the other room. Around 1860, the owners went up another story, using reinforced concrete. The *osteria* has been here for 100 to 125 years."

Construction for this building, like most in Venezia, involved driving wooden piles into the mud (which sealed the wood) and then building a foundation on top of this support. The church Santa Maria della Salute sits on 1,200,000 piles. That's a lot of piles.

The two families have not changed the interior of the osteria much since they took it over, other than to renovate the kitchen and storeroom and improve the washrooms. In addition, Emilio added the 60 framed photos on the wall from a collection of 100 old prints that a friend sold him. They come from two books published by Ferdinando Ongania, entitled *Calli e Canali* (1892) and *Calli, Canali, e Isole della Laguna* (1897). Ongania worked with many photographers to create a record of Venice and its islands, capturing daily life on the streets and squares in black and white. The photographers shot these photos on dry plate-glass negatives, coated on one side with an emulsion of gelatin and metallic silver, and first manufactured in the 1880s.

Al Bacareto also contributes some fun to the neighborhood. "In 2005, my brother-in-law had the idea to organize *una festa di quartiere* (neighborhood party), a dinner," says Emilio. "This happened a lot in Venezia many years ago. For the festa, everyone brought food and wine to share. We set it up on the salizada in front here—it's about 100-meters (300-feet) long. In the beginning, we figured there would be 70 or 80 people, but there were 220. It began to get a little overwhelming—we moved all the tables and chairs out of the restaurant to make one long table. There was singing and dancing, and we honored the elderly who were born and lived in this quartiere, San Samuel.

"It flowed smoothly, and that's difficult to do. We started to prepare at 4, at 6:30 it was ready, including the lighting. At midnight everything was cleaned up. It was a great success…this was September 24, 2005, and we redid it in September of 2006 and 2007."

In addition, Emilio's brother-in-law Meme organizes a fishing contest twice a year, an ongoing event since 1986. Everyone fishes off the island of Pellestrina, little more than a sandbar located just south of the Lido, with the prize going to—you guessed it—the one with the biggest fish.

While not an avid fisherman, Emilio has other hobbies: motorcycles, sailboats, and his house. He's especially proud of the 15th-century casa Veneziana that he and his wife have completely renovated—a big financial commitment. Fortunately, they received help from the Comune di Venezia because it was a historical building (there's a special law that provides funds for *lavori di restauro.*) The original owners of the casa, Avogadori, a family of judges, controlled the flow of money in the republic.

Life is good for the owners of Al Bacareto. Emilio's brother-in-law said to him the other day, "What a life we've made. Today, we've been here 35 years, and it still seems to me like the first."

For a wide range of traditional Venetian dishes, rustic Al Bacareto is the real thing. Eat in the restaurant, or stand at the bar and savor the cicchetti—especially the sarde fritte *(fried sardines) and* polpette *(spicy meatballs)—washed down with an ombra or two. This second option will save you some money, and you'll experience a fun, lively bar. Even though near San Marco, Al Bacareto's neighborhood offers a small taste of the real Venice.*

Pasticceria Didovich

Campo di Santa Marina 5908
San Marco
041 5230017
Open 7:30AM–8PM
Closed Sundays

*R*ight around the corner from the tourist throngs near the Rialto Bridge sits a *zona tranquilla* (tranquil zone), Campo di Santa Marina. "It's like another world here. Two hundred meters away—there's chaos," says Giovanna Didovich, a small, pretty, and extremely charming young woman whose family owns a *pasticceria* on the campo.

"The name Didovich is either Austrian or Dalmatian in origin," continues Giovanna, "but we have been in Venice for over 500 years. In Venice, there are many people with Austrian or Croatian surnames."

Giovanna's father, Italo Didovich, started this business in 1980. He began his career working as a *pasticciere* (pastry maker) at the age of fifteen, and, in addition to studying in Düsseldorf and Paris, apprenticed with Novak and Idelmo, masters in the Austro-Hungarian school of pastry. Of this tradition, it's said the dough on a perfect apple strudel is stretched so finely that a love letter may be read through it.

Italo worked his way up the ranks, *è venuto dalla gavetta*, as the Italians say—first opening a bakery that supplied baked goods for other shops, and then eventually moving to the campo. He expanded the current premises to what they are today, taking over a nearby *laboratorio* (kitchen) and shop front. This other location, their panetteria Gran Forno, had been a pasticceria for 100 years—the family added a bar

and began to sell savory pies and snacks such as *torta pasqualina*, made with ricotta, spinach, eggs, and prosciutto in a flaky pastry.

One kitchen generates everything that Didovich sells. "We use the best-quality products—no prepackaged or manufactured ingredients," says Giovanna. "We use the same ingredients they did 100 years ago, with the added advantage of the latest equipment. Our specialty is *dolce a lievitazione naturale* (sweets made with natural yeast), such as panettone and foccacia."

Big industrial bakeries use *saccharomyces cerevisiae* (brewer's yeast) to speed up the process of making dough rise. The result is faster, but not better, because there's no proper fermentation of the dough and the flavor suffers.

At Pasticceria Didovich, everything is flavorful. Here are some of the delicious pastries you should try (not all at once, of course): plum cake, tiramisu, linzer torte, *pasticceria salata*, *petits fours*, *pasticceria da thé*, *mille foglie*, *meringate*, cream waffles, and *charlotte di frutta*. For breakfast, you'll also find a big assortment of sweets to complement your cappuccino.

Sometimes Italo Didovich closes the laboratorio so he can work alone, and create. "He's working on a sacher torte right now," explains Giovanna. "He also thinks it's important to close from time to time and get organized so the staff can work better. My father is a great talent and he has a great passion for his work. At 67, he's the first to arrive and the last to leave. We have three serious, highly motivated young pasticcieri, *ragazzi in gamba* (savvy guys), who work directly with my father, plus there are seven shop assistants in the two stores.

Giovanna graduated from university in 1997 with a degree in *lettere antiche* (classical literature), which could have led to teaching or a law degree, but instead she put herself in the kitchen next to her father—a completely different world from reading Greek and Latin poets and philosophers.

"I have it in my blood, " she says. "I learned from him. This is hard work and a

hard life for young people. Now, I go to work late—5:30 or 6, but before I was at work at four in the morning, which meant I got up at 3am."

Her aunt works in the business, as does her mother, Laura, who she describes as "a column and a pillar." After employment as a head nurse for many years, Laura retired and came to help in the shop with administration, staffing, PR, and redecoration—a Jill-of-all-trades.

"I've noticed that when we have a problem with the staff, we argue among ourselves," explains Giovanna, an only child. "When we have everything agreeable here, it's d'accordo in the family. And the dolci (sweets) are more beautiful because they come out of the oven in a more agreeable atmosphere."

In addition to good coffee and pastry, Didovich serves its customers good will in the form of a smile and positive atmosphere—that's why a family member is always present to make sure you feel at home. And the regulars do indeed feel very much at home. They often leave a house key, the mail, or a message for a passing spouse. Giovanna can even point to the woman who was their first customer on the campo—she has come almost every day since 1980.

"In the summer, we put little tables outside—everyone sits and talks. People with their newspaper, croissant, and cappuccino. And during the afternoon, my mother and I sit outside. It's like a *piccolo salotto* (little living room). This is important for both the public and for us. Plus, it helps the life in the campo a lot," says Giovanna.

During the 1960s and 1970s, Campo di Santa Marina flourished with shops and activity, then came the depopulation of Venice—down to around 60,000 from a 1946-high of 170,000. And the shops became empty shop fronts. (For more on Venice's depopulation, see the section on Muro.) Lately, the Campo has made a comeback. According to Giovanna, "The shops have been refurbished. There is a good restaurant and a furniture store—they're all family run. There's also a nice hotel."

The Campo took its name from the Chiesa di Santa Marina (church of Santa Marina), built in 1030 and restored many times over the centuries—the last two in 1705 and 1754. By 1808, it was reduced to a branch office status for neighboring church Santa Maria Formosa, and in 1818, came the final disgrace—it was closed and used to sell vino. The wine vendors would profane the former holy spot, shouting from the front door, in Venetian dialect, "*Un bocal a la Madona! Un bocal al Santissimo!*"(A pot of wine for the madonna! A pot of wine for the most sacred). One account says that in 1820 the defrocked church was finally torn down; another claims that what's left of its walls form part of the Hotel Santa Marina.

Winter is the busiest time on the campo for Didovich—many traditional Venetian holidays occur during this time of the year and there is a *cultura di dolce* tradition of eating sweets in celebration. There's Christmas, Carnevale, and some lesser-known occasions.

One of the latter, *Il Giorno dei Morti* or *dei Defunti,* falls on November 2. It originally celebrated the brief return of the deceased to spend a little time with family (which may or may not be a good thing). Various sweets are part of this event, just as *le fave* (fava beans) were used centuries ago in the similar celebrations of the ancient Greeks and Romans. Some even believed that the souls of the dead were hiding out in the beans.

Nine days later, November 11th, marks the Festa di San Martino. Saint Martin began as a member of the Roman Guard and later converted to Christianity. He became revered for cutting his cloak in half to share with an old man during a freezing winter day. Shortly after his good deed, the sun broke through the clouds—and because of this, Venetians sometimes refer to the warm days of November as the *l'estate di San Martino* (the summer of Saint Martin). Traditionally, the Festa di San Martino has been a day when children go around to the shops, singing and asking for candy and cookies.

Mostly locals patronize Pasticceria Didovich. There may be some famous people in the mix, too, but Giovanna says she doesn't pay much attention to that sort of thing. Although, she admits to having writer Donna Leon as a regular. Leon pens the charming Commissario Brunetti mysteries set in Venice, where she has resided for more than 20 years. (In some of her books, Brunetti visits Didovich for a *caffé* [espresso] and a pastry.) Leon inhabits the other Venice—the simple, small town that most tourists don't even know exists. "In Venice there's not a great social difference between people. Everyone talks to each other," Giovanna says.

Pull out your map of Venice, and follow it (and your nose) to out-of-the-way Campo Santa Marina. It's not far—and it's molto tranquillo, as is Pasticceria Didovich, where you can sit outside on a nice day and savor fine pastry made by owner Italo Didovich. He's at the top of the pasticcieri pecking order in Venice, along with Giancarlo Vio of Marchini and Franco Tonolo. Pastry bluebloods, if you will.

Pasticceria Marchini

San Marco-Spaderia, 676
041 5229109
Open 8AM–5PM
Closed Sundays

*G*iancarlo Vio has lots of energy—he sizzles as he talks to you, speaking quickly, with a machine-gun delivery. And when the topic is pastry, you can almost see the smoke coming out of his ears. Early on, he channeled his creative drive into being a *pasticciere* (pastry maker), with a slight diversion as a messenger boy. At 18, he became an *apprendista aiuto pasticciere* (apprentice pastry maker) at a pasticceria called Dall'Olio. Italo Didovich, another maestro in this book (see the previous Pasticceria Didovich section), apprenticed there at about the same time. "I left when Didovich came, and he did his three years…I've known him since we were boys. It is very, very important where you do your apprenticeship. Aside from what you learn, the maestro transmits a passion for what he does. This frames us," says Vio.

With six siblings, a seamstress mother, and a father employed as a marine engine mechanic at the Arsenale, money was tight. Vio went right to work when he finished school. He says, "I chose to be a *pasticciere* because there was an opportunity. Like Didovich and my other friends, you give it a try, and, if you like it, you stay with it. Throughout my life, this work has given me great satisfaction. And it has always rewarded me."

From Dall'Olio, Vio moved to Pasticceria Marchini. It had always been his dream to work for maestro Ernesto Marchini, who was considered numero uno in Venice. He got the gig due to his skill and initiative. In fact, he says of himself, "If I hadn't been a *pasticciere*, I'd be an entrepreneur."

After two years with Pasticceria Marchini, Vio went to Feltre and Pasticceria Garbuio (at the advice of maestro Ernesto). From there, the next big jumping-off point was Switzerland: Vio took a job with the best pasticceria in Zurich. But life was a little more complex at this point—he had married the lovely Fernanda "Ferdi" Schenal.

For pasticcieri, Switzerland means "the big time" because the Swiss set the mark, especially in working with chocolate. They're recognized as the chocolate masters of the world. "Forty-five years ago chocolate was not well known or appreciated in Venezia," says Vio.

Life in Zurich meant another language and a very different lifestyle from Venice. The years in Switzerland were hard: long days, few holidays, lots of work; however, their jobs paid very well (Ferdi found employment as a hairdresser), and Vio developed expertise in all phases of chocolate production, the future specialty of Marchini. He eventually became *capo pasticciere* (head pastry maker) for the famous Zurich maestro, Ernst Angst. The Swiss punctuality, openness to innovation, discipline, and high standards rubbed off on the handsome young Vio.

In fact, if someone wants to open a café, pasticceria, or restaurant in Switzerland, they have to complete a course at the famous Richemont hotel school in Lucerne, where the standards are rigorous. "The Swiss are not like the Italians. No, with the Swiss, you have to do this and then you have to do that. And that. And that. When someone comes out of that school, they come out the right way," says Vio.

In February 1964, the most joyful event of the Swiss sojourn took place: the arrival of first child and daughter, Ornella Patrizia. All in all, the move north was, as the Italians say, "*Vale la pena*" (worth the pain).

But with the new arrival, Ferdi and Vio decided to rethink things and find a way back to Venezia after their four-year absence.

Enter the Colussi brothers with a job in the homeland at the same attractive Swiss salary. "The Colussi had seven or eight pasticcerie in Venezia and others scattered around the Veneto. They were a big company and a promoter of *baicoli*, a *biscotto Veneziano* (a Venetian cookie). I became *capo pasticciere* for Colussi. Later on, following the death of the *vecchio* Colussi… I don't know if it was a question of internal politics… but they closed all their locations. And became property managers, renting out their locations," explains Vio. After two years with them, Vio bought Pasticceria Regina on Via Regina, his first business. Soon Ferdi got involved, working as a *commessa* (shop assistant), and in 1967 their second daughter, Alessandra, was born.

Ambitious, talented, and a man in a hurry, Vio's next big move was to acquire his prize, Pasticceria Marchini, in 1974. Marchini had owned the business for 25 years, and after some heart problems, he leased it to his manager. Eventually, the manager gave the business back, Marchini put it up for sale, and Vio bought it. And for a while, the family juggled three businesses: Pasticceria Regina, the bar/pasticceria ai Frari, and Pasticceria Marchini.

Pasticceria Marchini was a fixture on Campo Santo Stefano for many years. This spade-shaped campo, near Piazza San Marco, but oh-so-far-away in its neighborhood atmosphere, became the site of an Augustinian convent, along with a church dedicated to Santo Stefano, in 1264. Thirty years later, Benedictines took over this convent complex. Lightening struck the campanile on August 7, 1585— it caught fire, melting the bronze bells, and collapsed on an orphanage housing sick children.

In happier history, Campo Santo Stefano served as a popular meeting place for Venetians, and during Carnevale, a strip of grass or *liston della maschera* was laid across it for revelers to strut their stuff. The *liston* usually appeared after 11PM and remained until the early hours of the morning. During this time, people flirted, flaunted, and generally pushed the moral envelope behind the anonymity of their masks.

After selling Pasticceria Regina and the bar/pasticceria ai Frari, the family concentrated on running Marchini from its original Campo San Stefano location until 2002, when they transferred to the Spadaria near San Marco. "We changed because the other business was *troppo pesante* (too much work). My daughters wanted a little different direction than before. They wanted to have another type of *negozio*, more a *cioccolateria* and a *biscotteria*. So we moved and reorganized the

business. It's less *impegnativo* (demanding) than the other place and its location is better for business," says Vio. Ornella handles the administration from the nearby office, and Alessandra looks after the purchasing and works in the shop.

Are there a few important things pasticcieri must know?

"Everything is important," Vio says. "However, this business is so big you can't embrace all of it. You have to make choices. A *pasticciere*, for example, that knows chocolate generally finds it easy to work with panettone, focaccie, pan d'oro, torte. Then, there are some who know chocolate and don't know any of these other areas. For me chocolate is a *complimento*, because I come out of the traditional pasticceria."

Along the way, Vio and Marchini have picked up a few awards. In 1975, he won the Oscar Italiano della Pasticceria. The year 1979 brought the Mercurio d'Oro, given to specially selected businesses that display dignity, integrity, creativity, and entrepreneurial spirit—and respect the laws of the marketplace. He also won the first prize, *Mattarello d'Oro* or golden rolling pin, for his Torta del Doge recipe at the 1989 Concorso Nazionale. This has become his signature pastry and one of Marchini's best sellers. It contains flour, butter, sugar, eggs, honey, raisins, walnuts, pine nuts, almonds, and rum—and is it yum!

As the name suggests, Torta del Doge is named for a doge—in particular, Andrea Gritti, the 77th doge of Venice, born in April 1455. Gritti came from a good Venetian family and spoke many languages as a result of living in England, Spain, France, and Constantinople with his grandfather, an important embassy official.

He had a distinguished military career, and was known as a great strategist. For example, after League of Cambrai members France, Spain, the Pope, and Holy Roman Emperor Maximillian ganged up on Venice, the republic lost most of its mainland possessions. Gritti reversed the situation by recapturing Padova on July 17, 1509. While Emperor Maximillian controlled the city, Gritti pushed a convoy of peasants and grain carts, with his soldiers mixed in, through the city gates and retook Padua, planting Venetian flags on all the towers.

In 1523, the politically astute Gritti became doge. He focused his time in office on ending Venice's involvement in the Italian wars and staying out of France and Spain's squabbles—and alerting the other western powers to the Ottoman threat.

Vio also received the prestigious title, Commandeur des Cordons Bleus de France, in 1990. Gastan Gerard founded the Commanderie des Cordon Bleus de France in 1949 as the guardian of culinary traditions and good eating. Representing excellence in a particular culinary field, new members present a thesis on a local and typical product. Vio did his on the *zaletto*—the raisin-filled lemony cornmeal biscuit of Venice.

Here are some high points from his presentation: During its peak, Venice sat at the trading crossroads of the world, with incredible riches and an abundance of raw materials. This facilitated the development of many arts and crafts. In particular, flour and wheat for bakers were available in great quantities, and the government encouraged their use to avoid spoilage and waste. The bakers of those days had only primitive ovens and strong arms, consequently they produced basic goods, such as the *zaletto*. Its ingredients were cheap, and easy to find in the *mercato*.

In the very old days, Venetians gave everything a nickname—and because these biscuits or cookies were yellow from cornmeal or *granoturco*, they became *zaletto*, which means "yellow" in Venetian dialect. The recipe used today has been around for 600 or 700 years. That's a long time.

According to Vio, *marzapane* (marzipan)—the delightful paste concoction of egg whites, sugar, and ground almonds—originated in Venice. The city marketed great quantities of almonds from Puglia, and, during the 1600s, local pastry makers used lots of them to create a specialty called *pane di San Marco*, which in Veneziano became *marzapan*, which in turn became Italianized to *marzapane*. Eventually, demand grew, creating a big business. Marzipan suppliers, concentrated on *Calle de la Mandola* (street of almonds), mixed large amounts of ground almonds with egg whites, sugar, and flour—using no oil because it would go rancid.

In addition to Torta del Doge and *zaletti*, Vio creates big cakes on commission for weddings and VIPs, including Lady Diana. He made a large intricate replica of the Tower of London for her 1979 visit.

Interested in taking a bite from a 747 wing? You could have, if you were among the guests at the premier of the Harrison Ford thriller *Air Force One* (1997), during the Venice Film Festival. Vio delivered a 30-kilo (66-pound) replica of the president's personal airplane to the Palazzo Pisani Moretta for the post-viewing party. (Erected on the Grand Canal at the end of the 1400s, and restored in the 1800s, the palazzo lists Czar Paul of Russia, Joséphine Bonaparte, and Joseph II of Austria among its famous visitors, besides Mr. Ford, of course.)

The movie community also tapped Vio for another bigger-than-life project—the construction of two elegant 30-kilo cakes for a party celebrating the release of the 2005 film *Casanova*, starring Heath Ledger. Construction is the appropriate term here because, as Vio says, "I make them in pieces, then assemble and decorate them on the premises." It can take anywhere from two days to a week. Over the past 30 years, Vio has gained the reputation as someone who can deliver on giant sweets like this—he's the "go-to guy."

When he's not creating pastry of all sizes, Vio spends time with his mostly Mercedes car collection: an SL190, SL300 Pagoda (with the Japanese pagoda-shaped roof), S320 for everyday use, a Jeep Grand Cherokee to handle snow and mountains, and his baby—a 1957 SL300 Gullwing. (So named because the doors are hinged at the roofline, and when opened, resemble a seagull's wings.) The car, one of only 1,400 of these unique automobiles left in world—took four years to completely restore. Each costs a small fortune. "Once in a while when it's a beautiful sunny day, I take it for a drive."

Vio's daughter Alessandra talks about how daily existence in Venice has changed. There's no more *la calma*—the Sunday tradition of buying sweets and spending time at home with the family. Now, Venetians leave town on their day off.

Giancarlo Vio continues contributing his pastry to this fine, old—and unfortunately—fading tradition. When asked about retiring, he says, "I still like what I'm doing." It will be hard to find someone who can follow in his footsteps.

Spend some time with your sweet tooth on the Spadaria in Pasticceria Marchini. Owner and pastry chef Giancarlo Vio is a legend. Come here for the zaletti, *the s-shaped* buranelli, *his signature* Torta del Doge, *and anything chocolate. There's no coffee, but who cares? You'll get coffee somewhere else, and often Marchini has a caldron of hot chocolate for tasting. (The prestigious—and expensive—Caffé Florian thinks enough of Marchini to serve Vio's brioche.)*

Trattoria da Fiore

Calle delle Botteghe
San Marco 3461
041 5235310
Cichetteria open 9AM–11PM, ristorante 12–3:30PM, 7–10:30PM
Closed Tuesdays
Closed from July 30–August 20

Not everybody loves Venice—in particular, the grumpy classicist Edward Gibbons, of *The Decline and Fall of the Roman Empire* fame. Here's what he said in a letter written April 22, 1765:

Of all the towns in Italy I am the least satisfied with Venice; objects which are only singular without pleasing, produce a momentary surprise which soon gives way to satiety and disgust. Old and in general ill built houses, ruined pictures, and stinking ditches dignified with the pompous denomination of Canals; a fine bridge spoilt by two rows of houses upon it. And a large square decorated with the worst Architecture I ever saw, and wonderful only in a place where there is more land than water; such are the colours I should employ in my portrait of Venice…"

Some would disagree, as writer Jan Morris does in a first impression of La Serenissima from her book *Venice*.

> It is very old, and very grand, and bent-backed. Its towers survey the lagoon in crotchety splendour, some leaning one way, some another. Its skyline is elaborate with campaniles, domes, pinnacles, cranes, riggings, television aerials, crenellations, eccentric chimneys, and a big red grain elevator. There are glimpses of flags and fretted rooftops, marble pillars, cavernous canals. An incessant bustle of boats passes before the quays of the place; a great white liner slips toward its port; a multitude of tottering palaces, brooding and monstrous, presses toward its waterfront like so many invalid aristocrats jostling for fresh air. It is a gnarled but gorgeous city… the whole scene seems to shimmer—with pinkness, with age, with self-satisfaction, with sadness, with delight.

Sergio Boschian, proprietor of Trattoria da Fiore, definitely agrees with Morris—he left a promising life as a migrant in Melbourne, Australia, because he missed Venice.

Australia had been starved for settlers ever since the first fleet landed in 1788, with 736 convicts. Fast forward to 1955, when postwar immigration reached one million, including 40,000 Italians alone, who went to the state of Victoria, mainly to Melbourne. Migration from Italy to Victoria peaked at 120,000 in 1971. Many new arrivals were single men, and most fit into the tradesman, production worker, and laborer category. These migrants or "New Australians" received assisted passage from the government—in other words, a free one-way ticket.

Part of this New Australian wave, Sergio Boschian emigrated from Venice in 1968 with his wife and young child. By 1973, he was living in East Coburg, a Melbourne inner-city suburb, and the family had grown to five—with the addition of children David and Lisa. Things were going well, except that Australia was a very long way from anywhere, especially Western Europe.

Then one day Sergio saw a film on TV that showed *vaporetti* (Venice's ferries) on the Grand Canal, and became very homesick. He sold his house, most of the family's possessions, and moved back to Venice. "To return by air, it was 2,045,000 lire for five people in total. To go by ship was 2,050,000 lire (US$3,400). Everything included. Two months on the ship seemed perfect. We went by ship," says Sergio. His ship, the *Galileo Galilei*, stopped in Fiji, New Caledonia, Panama, Spain, Greece, and the Italian ports of Messina, Napoli, and Genova.

Launched in April of 1963, as part of the Lloyd Triestino Line's Italy-to-Australia migrant service (along with twin *Guglielmo Marconi*), the ship displayed sleek eye-pleasing lines, a design later replaced by the boxy, floating malls of today. The *Galileo*

Galilei's maiden voyage took 156 first-class passengers and 1,594 second-class passengers from Genoa to Sydney. Fourteen years later, both she and the *Guglielmo Marconi* sat laid up in Genoa, victims of high fuel costs and competition from jumbo jets. This ended Lloyd Triestino's 140 years of passenger service.

Founded as Lloyd Austriaco in 1838, Lloyd Triestino became one of the world's biggest shipping companies by handling most of the overseas trade and passenger travel of the Austro-Hungarian Empire until 1918. At this time, its activities extended to four continents (Europe, Asia, Africa, Australia) with 62 ships.

The company's name changed to Lloyd Triestino in 1919, when its homeport of Trieste became part of Italy after World War I. It was devastated during the Great War, only to recover and have history repeat itself during World War II, when Il Duce conscripted most of its fleet for military service. By 1945, 68 ships were gone, 1,000 sailors dead, and only five ships remained afloat. Nevertheless, the company staged yet another comeback—and by 1957, the fleet numbered 31 vessels.

"When I got back here, I worked as a waiter in Caffé Quadri on San Marco," says Sergio. "I did that for ten years and then we had the chance to buy this place in 1984. There has always been a *tipica osteria* here since the late 1800s."

In those days, an osteria was someplace you brought your own food to eat and purchased their wine to drink with it. Often the owner served a bar snack such as chopped boiled meat, along with fried potatoes. He calculated that the wine purchases would pay for the free food. As insurance, the meat was highly salted.

"In 1925 or 1930, two brothers named it da Fiore. And since then, no one changed the name. And I didn't either," explains Sergio. (This da Fiore is not to be confused with the other one—the upscale and very expensive restaurant in sestiere San Polo.)

Sergio maintains a simple, tasty, and seasonal menu in the cichetteria or bacaro where you can, as they say in Veneziano, *andar a cichettare*, or slide up to the bar for an *ombra* and a nibble on *il pesce fritto* (fried calamari, shrimp, sardines), *le verdure fritte* (fried zucchini flowers, eggplant, peppers, artichokes). The sit-down, trattoria section of da Fiore features dishes that also reflect the seasons: *funghi* (mushrooms), *radicchio trevigiano* (elongated radicchio), and artichokes and asparagus from the island of Sant'Erasmo; along with the fruit of *la laguna Veneziana*—*rombo* (turbot), *sogliola* (sole), *branzino* (sea bass), *grancevole* (crab), *molecche* (soft shell crabs), *scampi* (shrimp).

In Venice, there's a simple trick to eating well: Eat what the locals eat—this means avoiding tourist-trap pizza and tomato-based dishes because *pomodori* (tomatoes) are not part of *la cucina tipica Veneziana*.

"We try to maintain a traditional Venetian cuisine. But sometimes it's not easy, because the customers want to teach us their habits. For example, it's easier to make dishes that have too much sauce like they do in America. Sauces that cover the flavor. Americans also want to squeeze lemon on their calamari fritte. That's not part of cucina Venezia. Lemon tends to hide or flatten the flavor, with lemon you destroy the sweetness of the fresh calamari. But we give it to them, if they ask for it," says Sergio.

David, who works in the family business, effortlessly picks up his father's train of thought, like a baton, "With the invasion of tourists it's hard to keep up the tradition… you feel the pressure. The problem: How do you keep the city alive without it becoming a large store or just a *città turistica*? It's easier to let the tradition go, and just cater to tourists."

Sergio and his family did cater to a group of tourists on one special occasion in 2005—the 60-year anniversary of the liberation of Venice. Sponsored by the Comune di Venezia, the event honored members of Popski's Private Army, a small, elite, and highly unconventional unit in the British army that specialized in sabotage and reconnaissance work in North Africa and Italy. Colonel John Campbell, the only remaining officer from the group, recalled the liberation in perfect Italian.

Popski's Private Army was formed in 1942 by eccentric Vladimir Peniakoff, son of Russian emigrants to Belgium, who raised him to speak English as his first language. (He also spoke French, German, along with some Russian and Italian.) While working as an engineer in the Egyptian sugar industry, World War II broke out, and already in his 40s, Peniakoff managed to wrangle a commission in the British army. He then formed a ragtag group of commandos, dubbed Popski's Private Army (PPA) by radio operators who had trouble pronouncing his real name. Attached to the British Eighth Army, Popski kept the PPA small—between 16 and 100—because he wanted to know each of his soldiers personally. He was less concerned about spit and polish (and proper uniforms), and more interested in results. If a recruit didn't measure up, they were fired—that is, sent back to their former unit. He developed a legendary esprit d'corps among the English, Scots, and French in his group.

Popski's Private Army moved about in jeeps armed with twin Vickers .303 caliber machine guns on swivel mounts. Because of careful planning and detailed intelligence gathering, mixed with a bit of swashbuckling, the group caused lots of trouble for the Germans, successfully pinpointing RAF targets and blowing up supply depots behind the lines.

Toward the end of the war, during an engagement with Germans at a farmhouse near Ravenna, Popski was shot in the right hand and his left hand was blown off. He was evacuated to England for convalescence and then rejoined the PPA in April 1945, just before the end of the war.

During the liberation of Venice, a landing craft pulled up to the Piazza San Marco and unloaded five PPA jeeps, and Popski enjoyed a exhilarating moment, leading the convoy in seven laps around the Piazza, one of the few times a motor vehicle operated in Venice.

Not far from Piazza San Marco sits da Fiore. Both father and son refer to their location in la parrocchia di Santo Stefano, a little outside San Marco, as a *ben*

nascosto—close but too close. The word *parrocchia* (parish) is a subdivision of the Venetian *sestiere*. It came about during the early days of Venice when the wealthy offered protection to their less affluent neighbors. As these communities grew, a church was constructed, and eventually, people referred to the area around it as a *parrocchia*. In 1741, there were 73 *parrocchie*, and, by 1807, the number fell to 40, and finally to 30, in 1810. The small and protected parrocchia di Santo Stefano sits in a loop of the Grand Canal— consequently, fewer tourists pass through because it's not a transit zone. You'll still find small shops, such as bread bakers and fruit and vegetable sellers, with the necessities of daily life.

"It's a zone that's still 50 to 60 percent Veneziani," explains Sergio. "The rest are foreigners who own apartments and live in them six or seven months a year."

David continues: "Italians from other parts of Italy also come to Venice looking for an apartment. They often buy abandoned apartments and redo them. It's not always a matter of an *investimento* (investment)—it's a matter of them loving the city."

Sergio's kids live outside of Venice because everyday life is easier and less expensive, and his sister still lives about as far away from Venice as you can get—in Melbourne, where she's been since 1971.

He hasn't been back since he left. Still, sometimes friends from the old days in Melbourne knock on the door—and one asked, after an awkward moment, "You don't remember me, do you?" Little by little, Sergio recognized the bald, middle-aged man sitting across from him.

These visits from another time bring back memories, but Sergio has no regrets about leaving Melbourne. For him, life in Venice is irreplaceable. "Walking around the streets is magical—when you see someone they say, 'Ciao.' It's like this all day. In fact, if you leave for a week and return, and walk around the street, everyone says, 'Where were you?'"

David continues: "People not only know each other, they know everything about each other. There are no secrets. If you try to do something on the sly, everyone knows."

"For someone who's born in Venice and grows up here, it's very difficult to live in another type of city," adds Sergio. "With Venetian life, like life everywhere, *c'e goia e dolori* (there's joy and sadness)."

Nice family, the Boschians—they laugh, interrupt, and finish each other's sentences, and genuinely seem to enjoy one another.

Go and visit Sergio Boschian and his family. Their trattoria/cichetteria is tucked away inside an area defined by the Grand Canal—and it's close, yet so far, from the crowded Piazza San Marco area. You can plan a nice sit-down meal with the traditional Venetian menu, or stand at the bar for a glass of wine and cicchetti. Sergio says, "In Veneziano *(the Venetian dialect), 'cichetti' means an* assaggino *(little snack) or to eat a little bit quickly. There are many definitions… in Trentino it means to drink a glass of grappa."*

· 3 ·

DORSODURO

Dorsoduro translates to "spine" or "hard back." Some claim the name comes from the geography—a finger of land with a hump of hard firm soil, higher than the surrounding area. Others say this sestiere got its moniker from the Dosduri family that came to live here from Padova. Earlier on, the area was sparsely inhabited because of its vulnerability to barbarian invasions. Doge Orzo Partecipazio put some of his "people" on Dorsoduro in 824 to help remedy this situation. They gained the nickname excusati *because they were excused from other jobs or duties.*

Cantinone "Già Schiavi"

Ponte San Trovaso
Dorsoduro 992
041 5230034
Open 8:30AM–2:30PM, 3:30PM–
8:30PM
Closed Sundays
Closed one week in August

After walking around in circles, all you need is another place that's hard to find. You'll have to get over it, because unless you know the city well, you always feel a little lost in Venice. But it's a "good lost." Half the fun is stumbling on something new and special, such as an out-of-the-way eatery with tasty fare, or two housewives talking across a narrow, serene canal—the Venetian version of chatting over the back fence.

Cantinone "Già Schiavi" is one of those places that's worth the hunt. The word *schiavo* means slave in Italian; however, owner Lino Gastaldi will tell you that slavery has nothing to do with this place—Schiavi happens to be the surname of the original owners.

They opened the business in 1890 and ran it until 1949, when Lino's father and two brothers bought it. In 1970, the father became ill and eight years later, he passed away. At that point, Lino and his wife Alessandra took over, and in the meantime, Paolo and Piero, two of their four sons, have joined them.

From the very beginning, wine was the drink of choice at Già Schiavi. Around 1890, the owners poured a local vino Veronese, a very light red, and also a stronger vino from Puglia, called *foresto* because it came from the less developed *meridionale* (southern) area of Italy. (Many inhabitants of this area came to Venezia around the turn of the century to sell wine and eventually open *osterie*.) During the 1930s, the owners of Già Schiavi made their own wine in *grandi botti* (large wine casks), which they kept out back.

Originally, the Schiavi family served a little food *al banco* (at the bar) along with their wine. The customers were poor and the fare was simple: sardines, half an egg, a slice of salami. "The habit of eating *cichetti* or bar snacks didn't exist then like it does today," says Lino. "My wife specializes in *cicchetti* because she has a passion for these things. She makes up her own recipes and has participated in *concorsi internationali* (international competition) for bar snacks. She even won a first place in Rimini. In the past 15–20 years, the popularity of *cichetti* has grown with tourism."

Not only the *cichetti*, but the wines have improved over the years. Lino and his family offer a selection of mostly local vintages—if you haven't tried some of the following, you should. (Remember Italian wines are best with food.)

Let's begin with Prosecco, a light, dry sparkling wine with a slightly bitter aftertaste—and nothing like that cheap spumante you may have drunk at one time. This is an enchanting drop, and Lino, along with most wine experts, says the best Prosecco comes from the towns of Conegliano, Valdobbiadene, and Pieve di Soligo, tucked away in the production area of northeastern Italy. Occasionally, you find Prosecco in a *spento* version—without carbonation. The best of the best Prosecco is unanimously recognized as Cartizze, from—you guessed it—Cartizze. In the old days, 80 to 100 years ago, Cartizze was less highly regarded than *Prosecco normale* (regular Prosecco).

Moving on to the reds, Amarone is a must drink. Smooth, full-bodied, and complex, it's made with grapes from the Valpolicella region, picked during the first weeks of October and then placed on racks to dry until January. The wine itself must age in small oak casks for at least two years before you get your hands on a bottle of it.

Raboso del Piave, another of the few Veneto reds that you can put away, has a robust flavor similar to a Barbera. Although highly acid and tannic in its foolish youth, it softens nicely with age.

"In Rome and Florence, they drink *caffè* (coffee) in the morning and afternoon," points out Lino. "However, here it's an *ombretta* (small glass of wine). We don't have cars like on *terra ferma*. We walk everywhere. You run into your friends and go have an *ombretta*. This has been passed down from generation to generation and it's a typical component of Venetian life. In the morning it's white wine, and in the afternoon it tends to be more red wine. This also became a habit for office workers

and blue collar workers—they take a break and drink a glass of wine and eat *cicchetti*."

You're wondering about the origin of the word *ombretta*, or *ombra,* which literally means "shade or shadow." Like all things in Italy, there is much variety here, so you can pick your explanation. Some say the oddball expression originated underneath the campanile in Piazza San Marco, where wine was sold by the glass from a barrel. As the sun moved, so did the wine sellers and their wine, in order to keep the wine cool in the shade. Another theory simply claims that the laborers and bricklayers took a break, out of the sun, *per bersi un bicchiere di vino* (to enjoy a glass of wine). Still others believe that *ombra* refers to the shadow of a liter bottle of wine.

The best way to find Già Schiavi, so you can down an *ombra* or two? Pinpoint the canal Rio di San Trovaso on your map—Già Schiavi sits at the foot of the Ponte di San Trovaso and almost across the street from the Squero San Trovaso.

This *squero* (boatyard) for gondolas, built in the 1600s, is the oldest in Venice. Think of it as the equivalent of an auto repair shop, with a difference—they also make gondolas from scratch, a time-consuming and expensive proposition, according to Lorenzo Della Toffola. He is the *gestore* (manager) of the Squero San Trovaso. The actual owner is the Comune di Venezia. Lorenzo, a no-nonsense Jeff Daniels look-alike, rents the facilities and contracts with the gondolieri to maintain and construct the gondolas. (At the time of this writing, Lorenzo had to move his operation to La Giudecca so the *comune* could renovate the *squero*, a three-year process.)

Lorenzo constructs the gondolas in a workroom/shed, open at one end. He's the *squerarolo* (master carpenter) and employs four workers. Building a new gondola begins with the 200-year-old molds that form the template of the boat. Every part of the gondola is made from a specific type of wood that has special characteristics. There's oak for the main supports. Transverse beams are made from cherry, with other parts using larch, fir, elm, walnut, mahogany, and small quantities of cornel.

"We make one or two new gondolas a year, and we have lots of maintenance work," explains Lorenzo. "The typical gondola comes in four or five times a year. It gets its bottom redone. It's washed, and then, every two years it's completely repainted. Because it's made completely of wood, it needs lots of attention. You have to dry it out completely so you can begin replacing pieces of wood for repairs."

When a *gondoliere* slides his craft up onto the *squero*'s sloping ground that runs down to the canal, it's the Ventian version of pulling into the auto mechanic's garage. A lot of the work is done in this open yard during the summer. In addition to the yard and enclosed workshop, the *squero* includes an attached chalet-like two-story building that houses living quarters. The facility was originally a small school for carpenters, and then at some point expanded into the *squero*.

"I began working here, doing little jobs and learning from an older guy, a real master. He taught me, and then when he retired, I came in," explains Lorenzo. "There are less and less young people interested in this type of work, even though there's lots of it. There is not a lot of time to teach them, and it's hard. They're interested in something easier that pays better. We work from 8 to 8… If I didn't like this type of work, I wouldn't be here."

In the end, a gondola is only as good as its gondoliere. And you have to be pretty good to handle a boat that measures 33-feet long and weighs 1,100 pounds, and do it with one big oar or *remo*. This tradition goes back at least 1,000 years.

Today, aspiring gondoliers must pass a 150-hour training course that includes art history, technical aspects of the boat, and a practical test on the water set up by the *Associazione Gondolieri di Venezia* (Gondolier Association of Venice). You need skill and stamina to control a boat this size in both choppy, open water and narrow, crowded canals. According to experienced (and handsome) gondoliere Fabio Zanetti it takes about three years before you're really proficient in a gondola.

After an aspiring gondoliere passes this exam, he has the equivalent of a gondola driver's permit, and he must follow strict rules that include how the gondola is fitted out and the width of the stripes on the gondoliere's shirt.

And this is just the beginning—once qualified, a gondoliere must obtain a license. The licensed number of gondoliere is kept at 425, with 100 substitutes. Recently, a law was passed that allowed the holder of a gondolier's license to sell it commercially. However, you must then hold it for five years before resale. It wasn't always this way.

"The law changed in 2005. A big mistake," says Vittorio Costantini, a barrel-chested, former gondolier. "This has interrupted the tradition of handing the

gondola license from father to son. You learn very young, in the gondola with your father. My father died while he was actively a gondolier, and there's a rule that the son takes over immediately when the father dies. The older brother is first in line, if he's not available, then the younger brother takes over the license, until the older brother is ready. If oldest doesn't want it, as in the case of my brother—he can renounce it, which he did in my favor.

"Also, the widow of a gondolier who has no children can choose who gets the license next, with the idea of keeping it in the family. At one time, you had to wait 14, 15, 16 years to get your first license. If you had a real desire to do this, you'd wait until it was available. I began as a gondolier at 17 years of age."

Vittorio worked as a gondoliere for 37 years and his son, Gabriele, followed in his footsteps. A few years back, Vittorio changed directions and opened Ca' Gottardi, an elegant and cozy hotel overlooking the Rio de Noal canal in the sestiere Cannaregio, which he runs with his daughter Tatiana and Gabriele.

Does he miss the life of a gondoliere?

"To be a gondoliere means a love for gondolas and means a love of Venezia," explains Vittoria. "I always say every dawn has its sunset. I like collaborating on this new project with my family—it keeps me busy, but not too busy."

Where there are gondolas, there is water, and sometimes in Venice there's too much water—as in *acqua alta*, the high tide that rises periodically between September and April and floods sections of the city. Look for photos of the *acqua alta* invading Già Schiavi on Lino's walls. "The high water comes to us a little later than the other places," says Lino. "And when it does come in, it goes into the small *magazzino* (warehouse) in back, up through a hole in the floor. We are a little higher in the front of the store.

"In 2000, we got 30 centimeters (12 inches) in the store—the kids could sail their boats on the floor. When we did a restoration in 1985, we did it in such a way that the bottles of wine are up off the floor, and the labels don't get ruined. Otherwise we can't sell the wine."

Constructed in about 1200, the building that Già Schiavi calls home was initially one story. (Look on the ceiling for an identifying mark etched by the original vendor of the support beams.) At some point in the building's history, the owners added a second story. Later on, it housed the office of a *notaio*—a notary who records the act of buying and selling property.

So, you've found Già Schiavi and settled in with an *ombra* and a plate of excellent *cichetti*. Time to sign Lino's visitors book—everyone is invited to add his or her autograph. If you browse it, you'll find some of the following high-profile folks.

In the political realm, Romano Prodi, *pezzo grosso* (big shot) and twice prime minister of Italy, swooped down with his *carabinieri* (paramilitary police) bodyguard. Joan Kennedy Smith, younger sister of JFK, in town for the Venice film festival, visited with fashion guru Giorgio Armani. Zera Yacob Amha Selassie, Crown Prince of Ethiopia, came here. He is the grandson of Emperor Haile Selassie.

You can read a short note from Italian pop singer Ornella Vanoni—known for her rendition of *Senza Fine*—who raced in to use the toilet. It says, "Grazie per il pepe." English actor Hugh Grant signed the book, as did Juliette Binoche, star of *Chocolat* and *The English Patient*, and Italian actress Mariangela Melato, known for her torrid work in the films of Lina Wertmuller, including *Swept Away* with Giancarlo Giannini.

Other people from the Italian film scene: erotic/avant-garde director Tinto Brass who helmed Gore Vidal's *Caligula* and stunt man and actor Giuliano Gemma, popular in spaghetti Westerns during the 1960s.

The visitor list also includes Daniele Scarpa, flat-water kayak medalist at the 1996 Summer Olympics (one silver and one gold)—who did not paddle up to the door. Singer Bono, on the other hand, did arrive by boat. At the time, Lino's son, drove a water taxi and picked up the superstar as his fare. He brought Bono by the canal in front of Già Schiavi so his brother Paolo, a big fan, could meet him.

But despite the occasional high-profile visitor, Già Schiavi is an unassuming place, in a *zona tranquilla* worth visiting, near the Galleria dell'Academia and the university.

Join locals and fellow tourists for an ombra and some of Alessandra Gastaldi's award-winning cichetti—such as baccalà with snippets of green onion, egg, and sun-dried tomato crostini, or panini loaded with mortadella or local salami. A photo on the wall shows the acqua alta at the 1.5-meter mark, but not to worry: Già Schiavi is on higher ground and it never gets much water inside.

Tonolo

Calle San Pantalon
Dorsoduro 3764
041 5237209
Open 7:45AM—8PM,
Tuesday to Saturday
7:45AM—1PM Sunday
Closed August

Franco Tonolo first saw Venezia when he was five years old. Every few months, his mother brought him the 20 kilometers from Mirano to visit her sister in La Serenissima. For him, this exotic world contrasted sharply with his home in the *campagna* (countryside)—and with itself. "I'd get a whiff of the marvelous perfume from the ladies in fur coats, and then we'd cross over a bridge and I'd smell the canals, which was sometimes not so good," says Franco.

His *nonno* (grandfather), Giuseppe Tonolo, started a pasticceria in Mirano in 1886. He had 10 children (who produced 33 grandchildren.) Of the 10, one died in World War I, two or three stayed in the business, and the others found work elsewhere because it was not possible for everyone to live from the pasticceria, even though it prospered.

At one time, there were no personnel other than family, including uncles, aunts, Franco's mother, his father Ennio, and his five brothers. Unfortunately, Ennio died

young, at 51. Franco's older brother took over, and later opened a second pasticceria in Venice. When 23-year-old Franco finished with the obligatory military service, his brother invited him to join the new location. This was 1959. Eventually his brother got homesick and returned to Mirano—"We were used to the *campagna*, the green, going around on bicycles…here there was none of that…it was just work and home." But Franco stayed.

"I'm 70, so that is 47 years," he adds.

The best way to describe Franco: an artist working with a palette of exquisite pastry. This tradition of artistry passed from his grandfather to his father to him and now to his children, Francesco and Giovanna.

Grandfather Giuseppe developed the recipe for the house specialty, a panettone-like focaccia that won a prize in Paris in 1909. At the time, his clients included many Venetian nobles who spent the holidays at their villas in the surrounding countryside. One of these enthusiastic patrons took a focaccia to Paris, on a whim (and unknown to Giuseppe), and entered it in the 4ᵉ Exposition Internationale d'Economie Domestique, Ville de Paris 1909. Two weeks later he brought back a diploma and gold medal for Tonolo.

The secret of this focaccia lies with the *lievito naturale* (natural yeast) that causes a slow fermentation, resulting in a better flavor—as opposed to the rush-job yeast used by industrial bakeries for their mediocre offerings. And there is nothing mediocre about this foccacia, with its unique marzipan and almond crust.

Few top-quality *pasticcieri* (pastry makers) exist in Venice today, and for good reason. It's extremely hard work. The average long and stressful day begins at 6AM and ends at 9PM. They enjoy no traditional holidays because during these periods they work their "buns" off. There's the busy Christmas season, and then Carnevale arrives in February when Tonolo's offerings include *galani*, light flakes of pastry dusted with powdered sugar, and *frittelle calde*, lemony-flavored fried dough sprinkled with sugar and sometimes filled with *zabaglione* or thick cream. Easter has its own pastry demands, along with the year-round production of focaccia and the following marvels: *torta di ricotta* (light ricotta cheese cake), *torta di ricotta con lampone* (light ricotta cheese cake with raspberries), *torta di mandorla* (almond cake), *torta meringhetta* (meringue cake), and a variety of *beignets* (French doughnuts)— *beignet chantilly con caramello*, *beignet caffé*, and *beignet cioccolato*.

Franco makes 50 different pastries; some are unique to him and some are not. His *krapfen* fits in both camps. The special recipe for his version of this marmalade-filled pastry came via a group of English officers billeted in Franco's hometown at the end of World War II. They patronized the pasticceria, became friendly with the family, and sometimes even had dinner at Franco's house. The officers also had their own German cook who eventually taught the Tonolo family how to make her type of *krapfen*.

"My mother was a good cook. This was 1946. I was ten years old," says Franco. "One of the English spoke Italian and I remember them eating chicken with a knife and fork. We ate chicken with our fingers."

Work does not abate on Sunday, the traditional day of rest, because Venetians traditionally bring home a box of pastries. Nor is Monday, the Tonolo official *giorno di riposo* (day off), actually a day off. "There is always something that isn't working… the fridge, and so forth. And when you're missing merchandise, you take the car and go to the warehouse. Myself, my wife, Giliana, and my children, we all have the same schedule. Everyday. It's difficult," explains Franco. At least the family does close during August for a well-deserved holiday.

For many years, after Franco closed the shop in the evening, he'd take a short drive to Mirano, circle the piazza, pass by his old house, and stop at the pasticceria to visit his brother. Then, back to Venice. He did this because, as he puts it, *"Dove passi l'infanzia rimane sempre nel cuore.* (Where you grow up always remains in your heart)." Little by little, the intense nostalgia for his birthplace dissipated, and he no longer performs this ritual.

These days, he blows off steam by taking a long drive. "When I need a break, I grab my jacket and *scappo* (escape) and go for a ride in my car—200 kilometers in a couple hours, up into the mountains. I go to Bassano del Grappa…Asiago… Cortina d'Ampezzo, stop for coffee, and then turn around and come back." Franco makes this circuit in his sleek, stunning Mercedes CLS-class coupe, the AMG version with a hand-built 507 horsepower V8 engine.

As soon as Franco turned 18, he got his driver's license, and cars and motorcycles have been his hobby ever since. The lineup over the years has included a

Yamaha two-cylinder bike, Fiat Cinquecento, Renault, Kawasaki 1100, Alfa Romeo, Ducati, Mercedes CLS, and a small scooter. He also took up sailing—in a five-meter (15-foot) catamaran. Unfortunately, it's no more big bikes or boats for Franco. He's has some heart problems and he's not supposed to tire himself out.

Tonolo's location, only 100 meters from Venice's University Ca' Foscari, guarantees a steady stream of students. This university is headquartered in a palazzo built by the powerful Foscari family in the mid-1400s. A more famous member of the family, Francesco Foscari—also known as the "sad doge" because of his long, expensive wars; the conspiracies against him; and the problems resulting from his irresponsible son Jacopo—had to resign his office in disgrace, and died a week later. This was October 1457. Giuseppe Verdi wrote an opera called *I due Foscari* (The Two Foscaris) about this tragedy, first performed in 1844.

In the earlier days of Tonolo, a wave of university students, most of whom lived outside the city, would hit every morning after being disgorged by the 8AM train. This morning rush has diminished due to changes in lifestyle: Many students rent rooms in the city and others commute by car. Instead of arriving all at one time, they scatter throughout the day.

Some American students, studying Italian and economics, rented a house nearby, and when they left, they did so with a tear in their eye, saying to Franco, "Tonolo is the best." They stayed in Venice three or four months.

"Most of our clients are Veneziani; however, we're well known in Belgium, France, and Germany. And there was a Swiss couple here this morning—*pensionati* (pensioners), *anziani* (elderly). When they arrive at the train station, they say, '*Andiamo a Tonolo, a mangiare una focaccia* (Let's go to Tonolo for a focaccia).' They come straight here, eat a focaccia and four or five pastries, and drink a cappuccino. It's their tradition. They've been doing it for about ten years. The Swiss are very fussy," says Franco. "We're outside of the centro, not near San Marco, but nevertheless we've developed a good tourist clientele. After a tourist comes once, they're no longer a tourist. They are our client."

You might recognize some of the following people who drop in from time to time: Massimo Cacciari, the current mayor of Venice; Renzo Arbore, well-known Italian musician, director, actor, writer, and all-around showman; and actor Bruno Ganz who played the Fuhrer in *The Downfall: Hitler and the End of the Third Reich* (2004). He also appeared in *Pane e Tulipani* (2000), shot in Venice, and in Wim Wenders's *Wings of Desire* (1987). Born to an Italian mother and Swiss father in Zurich, Ganz is the friend of a Tonolo client. Actress Linda Evans, famous as the character Krystle Carrington in TV's *Dynasty* (1981–1989), came here years ago. But Franco reminds you, "We don't give much importance to the name, it's the person themselves, and the friendship."

Both inside and outside of Tonolo, you'll discover lots of history. Franco came across something that he wasn't aware of when he restored the interior. As the workmen knocked down a wall, they found a beam with a brand or markings that indicated its age to be more than 500 years. It was the identical type used in the construction of San Rocco church, near I Frari, suggesting it was most likely "borrowed" from the construction site, a common occurrence over the ten years it took to finish the building.

The Campo dei Frari, near San Rocco, contains a *pozzo* (well)—almost every campo in the city had at least one, and sometimes as many as four. Surrounded by salt water, Venice had to get fresh drinkable water somehow. One method was to dig a *pozzo*, line it with impermeable clay, and fill it with sand and porous rock. Rainwater then filtered through the rock and sand into a cistern. At a predetermined hour, the person in charge rang a bell and opened the well so that women of the neighborhood could fill their buckets. It's estimated there were 6,000 wells in 1700. The city constructed an aqueduct between 1882 and 1884, which finally liberated it from a historic scarcity of potable water.

Regarding water quality and availability, Samuel Sharp in his *Letters from Italy…in the Years 1765 and 1766* writes the following:

> The frequency of diarrheas in this city, is another argument, that the water they drink is purgative; but perhaps one of the greatest consequences of these wells, is, that they do not contain water enough for a family in long droughts, which frequently happen in Italy.

When the rain failed or the water became polluted, Venice looked toward the Brenta River on terra ferma—and someone to supply the city with H_2O. For centuries, *acquaioli* (water sellers) happily provided the service at great profit. The Pesaro family, owners of sumptuous Ca' Pesaro on the Grand Canal, grew wealthy delivering sweet drinking water to a sometimes-parched Venice, much like Chevron selling oil today.

Another bit of history located on the Campo San Pantalon illustrates how the Venetians had their own way of doing things. When you face the Rio di Ca' Foscari canal, to your left, at the water you'll see the following inscribed in the wall.

Lunghezze Minime Permesse (Minimum length permitted)
Per La Vendita del Pesce (for the sale of fish)
Delle Seguenti Quantita (of the following quantity)
Barbon Tria Sardella Sardon 7
Branzin Orada Dental Corbo 12
S Oaro Botolo Boseghela Soaso 12
Lotregan Meciato Verzo lata 12
Lovo sfogio passarin rombe 12
Usate 25
Strega 5
Peogio 3

These measurements refer to a human standard, such as the palm of the hand or the foot. Using the human body to measure was quite common in the early Venetian Republic. For example, during house construction, the master builder or mason used his own foot to determine lengths. Since many of them had different shoe sizes, this resulted in great confusion all around. By the middle 1700s, to remedy this situation, the republic adopted a base measurement, roughly the same size as the meter, called the *passo Veneto*. Eventually, the Austrians instituted the metric system when they controlled Venice in the early 1800s.

In addition, Venetian clocks ticked to their own 24-hour day that began at 4 pm—a fact reflected in the design of the clock on Piazza San Marco's *Torre dell'Orologio* (clock tower). And, the Venetian calendar started on March 1, until Napoleon did away with the custom when he ruled La Serenissima from 1805–1815.

Whatever time you're on, it's always the right moment to stop by Pasticceria Tonolo. It's all good there, even though everyone works a little too hard. Nevertheless, Franco Tonolo says, "To me this has always been the *ottimo lavoro* (best job)."

At Tonolo, they take the time to make everything fresh from the best ingredients—as a result, they sell happy pastries. Where to start? Just close your eyes and point; you can't go wrong. But if you don't want to live on the edge, ask for a slice of their award-winning, panettone-style focaccia. The coffee is happy, too—each cappuccino comes with a smile drawn with cocoa in the foam.

· 4 ·

SAN POLO

This smallest sestiere includes the Rialto area and numerous winding alleys tucked into the biggest curve of the Grand Canal. Campo San Polo, part of this ancient quarter, once hosted bull baitings. It's also where a future priest of the Chiesa San Polo was discovered as a newborn in a basket. According to the story, a gatto (cat) pushed over the basket, and the abandoned babe began bawling. A neighbor raised the boy, and he eventually became the parish priest. He took the name Antonio Gatto in honor of his feline discoverer.

All'Arco

Calle de l'Ochialer
San Polo 436
041 5205666
Open 8AM–5PM
Closed Sundays and two weeks in August

When you cross the magnificent Rialto Bridge into sestiere San Polo, keep going down Ruga degli Orefici past the stalls and vendors, and take a left on the main drag, Ruga Vecchia San Giovanni. A little farther on the right, look for an alleyway with an arch (directions are not an exact science in Venice). Walk under the arch called Sottoportego dei Do Mori—*sottoportego* refers to the open passageway that goes under part of a building or house. There you'll see All'Arco, which translates to "at the arch."

This hole-in-the-wall bacaro is run by Francesco Pinto, a chatty man who serves up unpretentious and delicious vino and *cichetti* to a mostly Venetian clientele, and mostly at lunchtime, when you'll find All'Arco jammed.

Venetian-born Francesco's surname, Pinto, is Pugliese; his grandfather came from Puglia to sell *vini pugliesi* in Venice. At that time, 1892, Puglia, the heel of the boot, exported its naturally-high-alcohol-content (17 percent), unadulterated vino to many parts of Italy. Venetians drank it, and winemakers in the Veneto bought it to blend with less substantial local wines.

Some of this strong, dark wine was made with Malvasia grapes, originally from Greece. The Venetians first tasted Malvasia wine during the mid-1200s when they were busy running things on the Peloponnesian peninsula and in most of the Mediterranean. They "borrowed" vine cuttings and replanted them on Crete and Cyprus. From there, the vines made their way to Puglia and other areas of Italy.

Later on, the Pugliesi sold their Malvasia wine directly to Dalmatia— ironically, sidestepping the Venetians. Italian merchants also went to England and traded barrels of Malvasia (or Malmsy) for fine English wool, which they transported to Italy and Flanders, where it was woven and made into high-quality products. Around 1300, the availability of port and Madeira eclipsed the demand for Malvasia.

Eventually, Francesco's grandfather moved from selling wine to opening an osteria in Cannaregio, the first of many Pugliesi who came to Venice at the turn of the century to be *osti veneziani* (Venetian innkeepers).

"The osteria of that time was different than it is today," says Francesco. "It served as a meeting place for the family. They would bring food from home and order wine, and pass the evening like this. The osterias were often open from 6 in the morning to 2 in the morning. They offered a little food—*cichetti*, hard-boiled eggs, a piece of

cheese—and two or three choices of wine. According to the law, you can't sell that high-alcohol type of wine anymore. It's loaded with tannin and this is not good for you. It gives you a headache."

Many of these turn-of-the-century Italian wines had American roots (literally), because by 1900, phylloxera—a scourge of tiny aphids that attack the roots of the grape vine—had destroyed two-thirds of European vineyards. (The reason: In 1862, hapless French wine merchant Monsieur Borty imported American vine cuttings with phylloxera in the roots, and planted them in a Rhône vineyard. It spread like smallpox.)

While botanists were trying to discover the cause, the common folk came up with their own theories. For example, in Tuscany, some people blamed railroad tracks—saying the iron in the rails polluted the soil—and ripped them up. Others claimed God was punishing mankind for its sinful ways.

Strangely enough, the cause turned out to be the cure. The phylloxera aphid is native to North America, where it lives on certain types of American vines without harming the roots. Since these vines are resistant to phylloxera, someone came up with the brilliant idea of grafting European vines onto US rootstock. And, it worked. Eventually, the American vines had three roles: producing grapes on their own roots; providing graft stock—French vine tops on US roots; and parenting genetic hybrids.

Francesco explains that by 1923, the Italian vineyards had recovered and special laws were passed requiring that wine be made only with local grapes. One of the imported vines from those early days is the Clinton (no relation to Bill or Hillary), described in *The Simon and Schuster Pocket Guide to Italian Wines* by Burton Anderson as, "an outlandish American vine surviving here as an outlaw." It originated in the cool northeastern part of the Americas.

The Pinto family osteria evolved as people became more affluent. "The television came on the scene around 1950–1955, and my family's osteria was the first one in Venezia with a TV," says Francesco. "People didn't have one at home. TV was an attraction, and it would fill the place up."

This bacaro first opened about 80 years ago, and Francesco has owned it since about 1996. Before that, the family had three places: Francisco ran one, his father ran one, and his mother ran the other. They decided at a certain point to consolidate and sell the two bigger places because his parents were getting older and wanted to retire. Francesco says, "I got this smaller place, because I didn't want to work too hard." (That's a joke—he puts in a very long day.) Francesco's son has joined him at All'Arco, which makes him the fourth-generation Pinto in the business.

Ask Francesco about what he dishes out on a daily basis and he'll tell you that it depends on what is in the lagoon and in the garden. His descriptions will make your mouth water. In spring, the *pescatori* (fisherman) start bringing in *le moleche* (silent "l"). These tender little soft-shell crabs are native to the lagoon and caught for about a month in both spring and fall. Francesco serves them floured and deep fried. He's also partial to *le seppie* (small cuttlefish), the only member of the squid family found in the lagoon, which he stir-fries in fresh olive oil. And then there are the long and narrow, tender and fleshy *carciofi di Sant'Erasmo* (artichokes with dark purple leaves from the island of Sant'Erasmo). The small baby ones are harvested in late April and can be quartered and stir-fried in olive oil, garlic, and parsley; battered and fried; or eaten raw. The larger ones appear from May to the end of June. With a chunk of fresh crusty bread, and a glass of local wine, these delicacies make a simple, tasty lunch.

Artichokes aren't the only thing that comes from bucolic, serene Sant'Erasmo. This 12-kilometer-long isle, larger than Venice with a tiny population, serves as the garden of La Serenissima, producing many of its vegetables—such as artichokes, asparagus, tomatoes, eggplant, and red pepper. The salty clay soil gives the produce a distinctive flavor. In the old days, many gardeners used oyster and crab shells to keep the acidity of the soil in balance.

The nearby Tribunale di Venezia (courthouse) tries to keep the scales of justice in balance. During lunchtime, however, justice takes a break and you'll find a judge or two at Francesco's, along with officials and office workers, such as Giordano and Emanuela who commute an hour from Trieste to their jobs at the Tribunale. Mix in a few fish market vendors, butchers, shoppers, and pensioners—and you've got a typical crowd at All'Arco. Later in the day, people drop in for a snack and a quick glass of wine. "You're not likely to have a glass of wine that requires some degree of meditation…one that needs half an hour to drink," explains Francesco. "You exchange a few words, and leave."

One thing most Venetians are happy to exchange more than a few words about is their beautiful city. "Sometimes even we Veneziani discover something new when we come around a corner," says Francesco.

"It's beautiful, but it's not comfortable," he continues. "We're used to it because we're born and raised here. We're used to living with the lack of convenience. You have to carry all shopping by hand. You can't fill the car up with wine, produce, and *acqua minerale*. Instead people, especially the older people, use a little cart called a *carrettino*."

Of course, most Venetians have some type of boat, and Francesco's ideal Sunday involves his motorboat. He takes it to Burano, the island with the colorful houses located a 40-minute ferry ride north of Venice, and meets his fisherman friends who live there. They supply the fish; he brings the wine. It's the good life—Venetian style.

If you're in the Rialto area looking for a nice little out-of-the-way bacaro, All'Arco is just what you need. Don't be afraid to go inside, even if it's crowded and you don't speak Italian. Just smile and point—proprietor Francesco Pinto won't bite. In fact, nothing makes him happier than to have you bite into one of his delicacies and enjoy an ombra.

Muro

Rialto San Polo 222
Venezia 30125
041 5237495
Open 9AM–3PM, 5PM–2AM
Closed Sundays

Before this Muro, there was another one—the bar that Giacomo Zammattio owned with his partners, Alberto and Enrico Bertoldini, and sold to start their new venture. Everyone referred to them as *i ragazzi del Muro* (the guys from il Muro), so they decided to simplify things and recycle the name.

The new and improved Muro (which means wall) sits on Campo Cesare Battisti già della Bella Vienna near the Rialto, a busy area of the city except for this little corner. "It was semi-deserted, nothing much going on," says Giacomo.

Seizing a business opportunity, *i ragazzi del Muro* bought their present space, an abandoned two-story *macelleria* (butcher shop), and gutted it. Originally, the first floor served as the retail area, while upstairs was a big meat locker filled with meat hooks and huge sides of beef.

Once they had an empty shell, the partners engaged an American architect, Michael Reza Foroutan of Metaform in Los Angeles, to transform it. "I met him when he was here on Venetian glass business," says Giacomo. "We went out a couple of evenings and became friends. I showed him the space. He said he wanted to design

something in Italy because he wanted visibility here. He got the measurements before he left and designed it for us from LA via fax and email and telephone. He did a great job… very interesting and very modern."

They wanted to try something new with both the space and menu—something different from the other places they had owned (a pub and a cocktail bar), which were more traditional. So, in addition to opting for an interior design with clean flowing lines and huge windows, the three partners, all Venetians, decided to do just the opposite of many other bacari / enoteche / restaurants and focus on their Venetian customers. The light, airy ground floor contains the bar with its large selection of wine and *cichetti*. The second-floor, sit-down restaurant features a menu by Bavarian chef Josef "Beppe" Klostermaier that changes every week, based on what's available.

"*Nuovo veneziano* is written on our window," says owner Giacomo Zammattio. "For us, this means local fish and produce from the markets next door and wine from the Veneto. It's new in the sense that we try to go beyond the same dishes that you find everywhere. There are some restaurants that change their menu every 25 years—for example when the owner dies. It's good to maintain tradition, but that's not the job of this place."

Instead of the traditional *bigoli in salsa*, *spaghetti alle seppie*, *fegato alla veneziana*, *baccalà mantecato*, *sarde in saor*, you'll encounter the following unique and tasty dishes: edible flower/palm heart salad; *tonno crudo* (raw tuna) and *knori*; lasagna tossed in a dried tomato, broad bean, and scallops ragout; tempura with fennel and herbs purée; Argentinean angus sirloin; white chocolate mousse, lightly drizzled in maple syrup; or a selection of brie, pecorino, smoked ricotta, and asiago paired with honey and homemade jam. The owners' attitude toward their business is captured in the following quote by George Bernard Shaw: "There is no sincerer love than the love of food."

Another quote—this time from Doris Lessing—sums up their approach to wine, "Life is too short to drink bad wine." At any one time, you can choose by the glass from a wide range of 15 whites or 15 reds, and more than 100 different wines if you buy an entire bottle. Prices start at 2.50 euros per glass. This is a very good deal considering you'll pay twice that for a not very good wine at any of the many tourist spots in Venice. The most flagrant example is Harry's Bar where a glass of wine and a plate of pasta will lighten your wallet by about 40 euros.

Competing for local clientele (a shrinking commodity) is quite a challenge when you consider there are 40,000 people living in Venice, and a total of 60,000 including the surrounding islands. This equates to a loss of about 110,000 inhabitants since 1946 when the Venetians numbered 170,000. (In the first half of the 1400s, the population numbered 150,000, making it the largest city in Europe.)

The average loss is about 1,000 Venetians per year, often replaced by wealthy foreigners. You have to be committed to life in La Serenissima, as writer Thomas Mann described it, "half fairy tale and half tourist trap." The city is damp, with exorbitant real estate prices and rents, shrinking services, and the yearly invasion of 12 million tourists. Due to these factors, many Venetians *scappano* (escape) to *terra ferma* (as they call the mainland).

Giacomo describes his challenge this way: "In Venice, there are 20 to 25,000 *anziani* (elderly) 65 to 70 years old. That's one-third of the population, then there is 20 percent *bambini* (children). That leaves 10–15,000 people going to bars, restaurants, and bacari, but some of them stay at home with children, or for other reasons. So between the ages of 22 and 40, we figure there are only 2 to 3,000 people who are in circulation, which is why we hope that the tourists will eventually want to come here also."

There's a lot of history to draw tourists to this oldest section of the city, and when Giacomo talks about the glorious past of the serene republic his eyes light up, as with most Venetians. It was a world power for two centuries—comparable to New York, if it were a city-state, with the biggest businesses, the best artists, and the most sumptuous palazzi. The wealthy Venetian merchant families held commerce between East and West in the palm of their hand—a virtual monopoly. They made alliances with Arabs and Turks that were beneficial for business, and, consequently, their ships sailed around the Mediterranean peacefully. As writer John Julius Norwich puts it, "A people famous for centuries as the most skilled seaman, the shrewdest and most courageous merchant adventurers of their time."

Their ships carried Dalmatian and Istrian pine, iron ore, salted meats, grain, cereals, dyed cloth, Murano glass, leatherwork, and Chioggia salt to Alexandria and other Eastern Mediterranean ports. They traded for cloves, nutmeg, and coriander (used to flavor meat), along with silk, carpets, gold, precious stone, Cretan sugar and wine, Black Sea Caviar, raisins, Syrian Wax, perfumes—and slaves. All of this exotic fare they sold in Europe for big money. Their huge fleet also acted more or less as a navy, which they used to protect Byzantine and Crusader ports in exchange for exclusive trading rights.

Venice also conducted business with its own money. In 1284, Doge Giovanni Dandolo began minting the Ducato, later called the Zecchino. Highly regarded for its gold content and quality mintage, it became the coin of choice in the eastern Mediterranean and as far away as India. This lasted until the fall of the Republic in 1797.

Although its motto was "make money not war," Venice became distracted by Genoa, another powerful maritime republic, and became drawn into politics on the Italian peninsula. The two rivals fought four major wars from 1255 to 1381, with Venice finally coming out victorious. While Venice focused on Genoa, however, Turkish power grew in Asia Minor, marking the beginning of the end for La Serenissima.

The slide began with the Ottoman invasion of the Western Mediterranean and the Balkans, and ended with the ignominious handing over of Venice by the French to the Austrians in 1815. The city remained under their control until 1866, when it was incorporated into the newly created Italian state. One brief interlude: Venetian lawyer Daniele Manin led a revolution in 1848 and set up a liberal republic that lasted five months, eventually brought down by cholera, dwindling food supplies, and Austrian artillery. The latter included what some believe to be the first aerial bombardment—20 bomb-bearing balloons were floated over Venice. Very few reached their destination, however; a large number blew back over Austrian lines. (It seemed like a good idea at the time.)

The palazzo in front of Muro housed a *circolo ufficiali* (officers' club) for Austrian soldiers, where the top brass lived the good life with beautiful women, good cigars, and bags of money—hence the Campo's original name, Bella Vienna. This has since been amended to Campo Cesare Battisti già della Bella Vienna and means "Campo Cesare Battisti formerly Bella Vienna," but everyone still refers to it as Campo Bella Vienna.

At this point, you might ask, "Who exactly is Cesare Battisti?" Well, Signor Battisti was an Italian patriot from Trentino, part of the Austro-Hungarian empire at the time of his birth in 1875, but still very much Italian in language and culture. Battisti grew up in a time when Italians wanted Trentino, along with Trieste and Istria (the area near Trieste), to be reunited with the rest of Italy following *Il Risorgimento*—the movement that unified Italy in the 1860s. These separated areas were referred to as *Terre Irredenti* (unredeemed lands).

At university, Battisti became a Socialist, and eventually entered politics, serving on the Austrian Parliament in 1911. He and Mussolini were friends during the latter's Socialist period. Believe it or not, Il Duce was initially more of a pacifist, but the pro-war sentiments of Battisti and other leftists turned him, and he embraced the aggressive stance of a pro-war nationalist. While Battisti helped start Mussolini down this road, most likely he would have been upset by Il Duce's final destination.

He never lived to experience the full bloom of Fascism. Battisti enlisted in the *Alpini* (the Italian Alpine Corps) to fight Austria during World War I, and was captured in July of 1916. Condemned to hang, he asked to be shot instead, so as not to dishonor the uniform. The request was granted (sort of): The court gave him a set of civilian duds from a used clothing store. During the first attempt to hang Battisti, the rope broke—according to tradition the sentence should have been commuted. Instead, the hangman got a new rope and, ending a very bad day for Battisti, finished the job.

It's ironic that the campo was named after two such extremes: Austrian officers living it up and an Italian patriot executed by the Austrians.

Muro changes personalities many times during the day. In the morning, between 10AM and noon, pensioners meet their friends to drink, smoke, and play cards. They make the rounds of about 15 bars within 300 meters.

"In the morning, they say *'un bianco o un rosso'* (a red or a white). They like it cheap and light," says Giacomo. "For a year, I serve them cabernet franc, and then change to merlot, and a little later, Sangiovese because it is young and light. And they had no idea. They want it cheap and not very strong because they drink a lot of it. The average is six or seven glasses each, and the percentage of alcohol is around 11 percent. They're not complex wines. Sometimes I sell a case of this type of wine in the morning, served by the glass." (These people must have the toughest livers in the world.)

At noon, the typical pensioner clears out and heads home for lunch. After which, he usually has a long nap—much to the delight of his wife because this keeps him out of her hair for a chunk of the afternoon.

The lunchtime Muro fills up with *pendolari* (commuters) who come to Venice for work, along with locals and some tourists, and then it grows quiet in the afternoon.

Once again, in the evening, the campo is full of life, thanks to Muro and four or five other bars and enoteche that have followed its lead. If you come by around 7PM, you'll find a *punto di ritrovo* (gathering place), a happy island of 70 to 80 people (25 to 45-year-olds) crowded in front of Muro, enjoying a spritz or a glass of wine. Sometimes this is a mixed blessing. "Most American tourists who pass by and want to eat dinner won't stop because this crowd scares them. They don't know about the dining room on the second floor. It is very difficult to have a bar and restaurant together because you're always worrying about one or the other," says Giacomo.

When asked about how he got his experience, Giacomo explains that he began in the early 1990s in a place called Le Bistro de Venise, which bases its historical and creative menu on old Venetian recipes (from 1400–1700), with ingredients as authentic as possible. He didn't attend a *scuola alberghiera* (culinary and hotel school), but instead, he says, "I drank a lot of wine and learned the business by doing it. On the street, so to speak. In fact, I'm not a good waiter. I'm not a good chef. But I am a good host. However, I have the capacity to do all of this if I need to, because in Venice you have to be able to do a little bit of everything."

When you're near the Rialto, go to Muro and drink wine in the morning with the pensionati *(pensioners). Or grab a nice lunch. Or, during the early evening, hang out with the younger crowd out front in the Campo. After a Spritz or two, check out the dinner menu in the sleek grey-and-black second-floor dining room. The food is excellent. As Virginia Woolf put it so well, "One cannot think well, love well, sleep well, if one has not dined well." You can also head over to the new Muro Pizza e Cucina on Campiello di Spezier in sestiere Santa Croce and try out the pizza kitchen.*

Osteria al Garanghelo

Calle dei Boteri
San Polo 1570-1571
041 721721
Open Thursday–Tuesday,
10AM–8:30PM
Closed Sunday evenings &
Wednesdays; Closed Sundays
& Wednesdays during July &
August; Closed a few weeks in
January & August

Renato Osto has developed *cucina veneziana* "light" to an art form. He tries to cook with very little salt, fat, and sugar. His secret weapon: a fast, versatile, and efficient combination steamer/convection oven that steams his homemade pasta, and cooks many of the other dishes with either steam or gas.

In the morning, he makes pasta and about 12 kilos of bread—a different flavor every day, including fennel, onion, olive, celery, and rosemary. "I also make the *dolci* (sweets) in the morning. We don't use sugar or eggs, not even in tiramisu. This makes it very light. One of our specialties is *budino del doge*, made with cream, amaretto, and mascarpone cheese. Another is *salami cioccolato*," says Renato. It's worth a visit to Osteria al Garanghelo just to taste these last two masterpieces. Somehow, Renato manages to create a rich creamy-tasting dessert that doesn't leave you saying, "Oh my god, I can't believe I ate the whole thing."

Renato's homemade, very thin *patatine* (potato chips) are another specialty, albeit a dangerous one because you can easily consume an entire basket of these tasty devils all by yourself. "We offer them to people when they drink an *ombretta* or a spritz." An industrial potato peeler, resembling a small robot, peels 200 kilos of potatoes per week. In this case, Renato breaks the rules, using oil and a little salt to create his signature snack.

The following list of exceptional dishes gives you a place to start with the menu: *gamberoni in saor*, *vongole al vapore con olio e whisky* (steamed clams with olive oil and whiskey), *polpette al vapore con pomodoro, vino, e peperoncino* (steamed meatballs with tomato, wine, and red pepper), *fagioli all'uccelletto con pomodoro, rosmarino, e peperoncino* (white beans with tomato, rosemary, and red pepper), *pasta con spezzatino*

di vitello (veal pasta), *spaghetti in salsa di sarde* (spaghetti with sardines), and *radicchio tardivo di Treviso con pancetta* (radicchio roasted with Italian bacon). The latter combines Italian bacon with the more zesty, pleasantly bitter *tardivo* variety of radicchio, an elongated, red-leafed, white-veined type of chicory, available from late November through the winter.

You might also want to consider two more sweet temptations—*crema pasticciera con frutti di bosco* (custard with blueberries, blackberries, and raspberries) and *mascarpone con cioccolato* (mascarpone cheese with dark chocolate).

Renato learned to cook by experimentation, when he owned a small bar, and from other good chefs. He and his business partner, Annalisa Mila, opened Osteria al Garanghelo in 2003 after restoring an old bakery to fit their vision of a classic *osteria veneziana*. They customized the kitchen and constructed an antique-style *bancone di legno* (wooden counter) with a shelf behind it to hold numerous 28-liter wine casks. They also hung tapestries and paintings capturing moments of La Serenissima's history on the 1,000-year-old, 60-centimeter-thick walls. "We thought a lot about everything," says Renato. "We've known each other for a long time. We opened this together to see how it would go—and it's gone well."

Italian tourists, foreign visitors, and Venetians patronize Renato and Annalisa's osteria. This latter group includes the versatile Lino Toffolo, stage and screen actor, singer, and cabaret performer. Born in 1934, Toffolo wrote, directed, and starred in the first Venetian-dialect film, *Nuvole di Vetro* (2006).

At the end of the day, Renato has just about enough energy to drag himself home and into bed. He spends Sunday, his day of rest, on the sofa gathering his energy for Monday and the job he loves.

Before this venture, Annalisa worked in accounting, and Renato did a number of things, including a stint as typographer for *Il Gazzettino*, the Venice daily newspaper. (Typography is the art of print, and typographers design the look of type on the printed page. In the modern digital world, typographers choose the best fonts, print, and lettering type for each particular job, such as books, magazines, the Internet, and other computer-related projects.) You may not know this, but Venice printed half the world's books in 1500—there were a total of 450 printers, publishers, and booksellers, many on the cutting edge of the printing arts.

Here are a few:

Aldo Manuzio (1450–1515), a Venetian printer and humanist, published the complete works of Plato and five volumes of Aristotle. He attracted the best scholars, proofreaders, and typesetters, and had a positive influence on Venetian publishing houses. Venetian books were in demand all over Europe.

In 1501, he printed the first book with Italic type, which delivered a higher character count for more legible type in less space. He also published the first "pocket book" of non-church literature—an edition of Virgil. Printers all over Europe copied his use of Italic type and small format.

Alessandro Paganini printed the first Arabic-version of the Quran in 1537, probably for export to the Ottoman Empire. He shot himself in the foot, though, by doing a sloppy job, with many errors and poorly legible type. The book was not a bestseller—it's believed the Ottomans confiscated and destroyed most copies, and the Vatican burned the remainder.

Another printing milestone centers on pyrotechnics (the fire-using arts). Vannuccio Biringuccio (1480–1539) published the first comprehensive book on this topic, including sections discussing metallurgy, mining, gunpowder, military defense, and fireworks.

You might be interested to know that Osteria al Garanghelo sits on the edge of Ca' Rampani, an area where the city fathers moved all prostitutes in 1360. *Carampana*, a local term for "whore," originated here. Under the scrutiny of six custodians, *le meretrici* (another word for "prostitutes") could work this centralized area everyday except important church holidays. They often displayed their wares on the nearby, and aptly named, Ponte delle Tette (bridge of tits).

In spite of the ladies' availability, homosexuality (or *sodomia*) was on the rise during the 1600s. The city government decided to combat this "scourge" by encouraging *le meretrici* to appear topless from their open windows. It's not clear what effect this had; nevertheless, in their infinite wisdom, the city fathers hedged their bets with a 1644 decree, lest things get out of control. It stated prostitutes could *not* do the following things: pay more than 100 ducati in rent; go around the

city in a boat with two oars; travel on the Grand Canal during business hours; enter a church on a feast day or during services; wear gold, jewelry, or real or false pearls; testify in criminal trials; or bring deadbeat clients to court.

Some popular "working names" for prostitutes in the 1600s were Damo, Elena, Fillide, Flora, Frine, Imperia, Laura, Lavinia, and Lucrezia. Needless to say, these were not popular monikers with the Venetian middle and upper classes.

If you like tasty, healthy, and mostly light fare, then get on over here. Chef Renato uses very little salt, sugar, or oil—and you'd never know it. He fools you with the treasure chest of herbs and other secrets hidden up the sleeves of his chef's jacket. It's worth a visit just to sit at the bar with uno spritz *and his homemade* patatine *(potato chips). In addition to the 10 counter seats, there are 24 more inside and 20 outside. Lunch goes from 11:30AM to 2PM and dinner 6 to 8:30PM; snacks and drinks, 10AM to 8:30PM. The Veneziano word "Garanghelo" means to be out in the countryside eating and drinking, laughing and joking.*

Osteria al Diavolo e l'Aquasanta

Calle della Madonna
San Polo 561/B
041 2770307
Open 9:30AM–11PM, Wednesday to Sunday
9:30AM–late afternoon, Monday
Closed Tuesdays

*I*n the old days, they ate almost every part of an animal. This is reflected in the *cucina povera* of Venice: *testina di vitello* (calf's head), *trippa* (tripe), *musetto* (boiled pork sausage), *rumegal* (morsels of boiled cow stomach dressed with salt and oil), *barbossi* (chin), and *nervetti* (boiled veal tendons). Some of this takes a little getting used to, and Osteria al Diavolo e l'Aquasanta provides the ideal place to initiate yourself. Mid-morning, owner Silvano Mazzarioli serves these *piatti* (dishes) to eager locals at the bar.

His location near the Rialto Bridge has been many things, including a storeroom, a laundry, and a kitchen of sorts. Fifty years ago, vendors prepared *cucina povera* dishes here and peddled them as energizing mid-morning snacks to laborers working in the nearby *mercato*.

"I work with my signora, Anna Banditelli. She comes at 6AM and starts cooking. She learned from good local cooks and worked in many places around Venice," says middle-aged Silvano, a gravelly voiced, salt-of-the-earth type. "She has a passion for the kitchen. I'm very happy with her, and very proud."

In addition to *cichetti* and Venetian cuisine such as *bigoli in salsa, fegato alla veneziana, baccalà condito con algio e prezzemolo,* and *seppie in nero,* Diavolo e l'Aquasanta serves seasonal specialties. November is the month for *radicchio rosso di Treviso* (the long radicchio), and on November 21, the traditional *castradina,* a very time-consuming dish made from smoked and boiled mutton, cooked with cabbage and onion.

This date also signifies the Festa della Madonna della Salute, commemorating the end of the 1680–1681 plague. The island city managed to escape the scourge, until it received some ambassadors from its plague-ridden neighbor, Mantova. In spite of quarantining the Mantuans on the island of San Servolo, a carpenter in the group fell sick and this parlayed into devastation for the city, which ended up losing about a third of its population. The situation became so desperate that the Venetians turned to prayer, holding a three-day vigil around Piazza San Marco and beseeching the Virgin Mary to save them. Suddenly, the progress of the plague slowed, and, in two weeks, it ran its course and disappeared.

To give thanks, Venice built the church Santa Maria della Salute (Holy Mary of Health). Every year, on November 21, the city constructs a temporary bridge on pontoons (originally on gondolas) that carries pilgrims across the Grand Canal to the church, where they light a candle for good health. *Castradina* is eaten in honor of the Dalmatians—the only people to provide Venice with food (especially mutton) during its 18-month self-isolation from the plague.

Something more fun to eat during this festa, especially for *stranieri* (foreigners), are the *frittelle calde*—lemony-flavored fried dough with sugar—sold from booths lined up along the Rio Terra di Catecumeni. They're so incredibly light you'll probably want to eat at least two.

The best way to make sure you get a good meal in Venice, where it's so easy to get a very bad one, is to stay out of restaurants geared to tourists, and order Venetian specialties. Avoid the ubiquitous pizza and other tomato-based dishes. "Long ago, the tomato did not exist in Venice—it arrived later from America—so the classic *cucina veneta* does not have tomato," says Silvano.

He began as a waiter in a Venetian trattoria when he was 14 and more or less grew up in the business. He says, "I learned what people want and what they eat." When the idea to open his own place came to Silvano, serendipity struck—a friend told him about an empty *magazzino* (warehouse space), and he decided to make the move.

How long did the renovations take Silvano? Too long! He had to contend with both construction problems and labyrinthine Venetian bureaucracies with names like Magistrato delle Acque and Magistrato della Salute. The city has many requirements; for example, in an establishment such as Diavolo e l'Aquasanta there should be one bathroom for every 20 seats; 25 seats require two bathrooms. Also, the septic tank must be large enough to handle activity from the osteria.

It's difficult to work in a damp, old, cramped city like Venice. Everything comes in and goes out by water—even the contents of Silvano's septic tank. Twice a year a big boat comes to pump it out.

Often the crafts that service Venice are specially designed, such as the compact garbage boats. It's actually fun to watch how they operate, because most people never experience garbage collection like this. The *operatore ecologico*, a bureaucratic (and green) euphemism for a trash collector, collects piles of trash in big metal carts from strategic spots along the canals. A crane from the garbage boat empties the cart into its hull, and then the crane and the cabin fold neatly into the deck.

"If you do work that is *lavori di ordinaria manutenzione*, you can go ahead, but if it's *lavori di straordinaria manutenzione*, you have to get a *permesso*," explains Silvano. "You can't just do what you want and knock out a wall. In a city as old as this, you have to follow the rules. You present your plans and then they approve them. And then it's stop and start. You need balls to do this. Because it is not easy."

Silvano stopped work for six months—paying rent, earning no income—as he awaited approval for a specific *permesso* (permit). Finally, at the eleventh hour, when everything came together, the various inspectors "inspected" to see that everything was done to their liking. If not, he couldn't have opened. "You have to be patient," says Silvano.

The interior looks much older than it is—Silvano designed it for this effect. He's especially proud of the artisan-constructed *banco* (counter), and also the unique sign hanging outside his front door. He conjured up the osteria's name by combining his nickname as a water taxi driver, *il diavolo* (the devil), and the Venetian nickname for wine, *aquasanta* (holy water). Two of his friends, Guida Fuga and Lele Vianello, illustrated the figures on the sign—a fat monk with a barrel pouring wine into a goblet held by a devil—and executed the graphic design.

You'll notice the influence of comic book art; both Guido and Lele collaborated with Hugo Pratt (1927–1995), considered one of the greats in the world of comic book artists for his ability to mix fantasy, graphic freedom, elements of literature, and exotic surroundings. Pratt led a peripatetic life, living in Rimini, Ethiopia, and then Venice when he was young. After World War II he worked in Argentina, England, and Italy. His best-known work, the *Corto Maltese* graphic novel series, follows the adventures of Corto, born of an English father and Spanish gypsy mother, as his seafaring life takes him around the world in the early 20th century. Milt Caniff's comic strip *Terry and the Pirates*, with its chiaroscuro approach to illustration, greatly influenced Pratt, who in turn set the tone for graphic novels to follow.

Guido Fuga contributed graphics for Pratt works such as the *Scorpions of the Desert*, and Lele worked on Pratt science fiction stories in *Venezia 7*, *Sinbad*, and *Il Mago*. In addition, the two collaborated with each other on a book entitled, *Navigar in Laguna, fra isole, fiabe e ricordi* (*Sailing across the Lagoon, among islands, fairytales, and memories*), a travel book that visits all the islands of the Venetian lagoon, and also on a second book, *Testimonianze di un Viaggio Straordinario* with watercolor illustrations capturing Marco Polo's exotic travels.

Another friend from the visual arts world, photographer Gianfranco Tagliapietra, gave Silvano photos from his private collection, some of which are in Tagliapietra's book *Lidhollywood*, chronicling the *Mostra del Cinema di Venezia* or Venice Film Festival on the Lido from 1959–1970. A selection of these framed prints hangs on the back room wall.

For twelve days at the end of August and the beginning of September, the Mostra dominates the ocean esplanade between the Excelsior Hotel and Hotel des Baines. It started in 1932 and is the oldest film festival still in existence. Tagliapietra captures its spirit with black-and-white photos from the *La Dolce Vita* period through wild-

and-wooly 1970. You'll see a youthful, annoyed George Hamilton interrupted in the barber's chair; *Hercules* star Steve Reeves accompanied by a beautiful French starlet; the smiling and very young Vittorio Gassman, Silvana Mangano, and Alberto Sordi; actor Richard Egan, dripping testosterone; and the threesome of film producer Marina Cicogna with famous directors Luchino Visconti and Federico Fellini.

Photos on the walls in the main room of the osteria show Silvano's father as a fit young man rowing in the Regata Storica during the early 1930s. Held on the first September every year since 1825, except for during World Wars I and II, this gala festival has two components—a historical procession and the regatta races. Competitors race standing up, Venetian style, in four divisions: two-oar *pupparini* boats for young people 17 to 20; *mascarete* boats with two female rowers; large *caorline* boats powered by six men; and championship *gondolini* boats for two male rowers.

There's also a photo of Silvano's mother and father, a handsome couple at the Lido di Venezia. "I think it was before they were engaged. She was from Poggibonsi in the Provincia di Siena and knew how to weave the straw for the Tuscan wine flasks," explains Silvano.

"My father worked in Venice, transporting wine barrels around in boats. The company he worked for hired my mother because they needed someone to weave straw baskets. And they met each other there. They were married here in Venezia. She had triplets, but one died in childbirth, so there's only my fraternal twin and me. They were both 40 when they were married. My mother had three children from her first husband. My father was a bachelor… *faceva la bella vita* (He was living the good life). From my father, I learned to be humble and to be true to myself. He was quiet and an exceptional person. He had a big heart. No money, but lots of love."

"I have a philosophy about this place, and life," he continues. "It's like the boat with my father and his friend in the regatta. Two rowers—one pushes and the other steers so you don't go the wrong way. If they don't agree and both want to steer, it doesn't work. The boat goes in circles. With me and my signora, one pushes and the other *governa* (steers)."

Silvano has a son in his 30s and his signora, Anna, has two children and two grandchildren. He refers to her as *una donna stupenda* and says, "When I met her, my life changed completely."

You can order a lot or a little—either way, it's okay with owner Silvano Mazzarioli. He just wants you to be contento. *Stand at the bar and eat* polpette *(fried meatballs), or sit down with a plate of* sarde in saor *(sardines marinated in vinegar, onions, pinenuts, and raisins) at one of the long shared tables and make some new friends.*

Rizzardini

Campiello dei Meloni
San Polo 1415
041 5223835
Open 7AM—9:30PM
Closed Tuesdays and in August

On August 30, 1742, the doge issued a decree prohibiting the use of *la bestemmia* (cursing) in half a dozen *Posti di Scaleter*, or bakeries, including this one on the busy Campiello dei Meloni. As early as 1300, this *campiello* (small square) was a depository for melons—hence the name. Merchants would store their cantaloupe here and later move them to the Rialto market, which was a straight shot by street with no bridges in between.

At the time of the doge's decree, bakers were called *scaleteri* because they specialized in a cake that resembled a *scala* (ladder), often used for weddings. A copy of the doge's decree hangs on the wall inside the door of Rizzardini.

Why did the doge establish bakeries as curse-free zones? Probably due to upper-class patrons inside and heavy foot traffic outside. Only the wealthy could afford sweets, which they purchased on special occasions such as religious holidays, marriages, or baptisms. Consequently, in those days, if you had the uncontrollable urge to let fly with an expletive or two, your best bet would be to do it well clear of any pastry shop.

The *scaleteri* followed certain rules. For example, they were not allowed to sell pastry without a proper oven; in addition, their product had to be sold within a certain period of time, or thrown out. In the year 1713, the Venetian *scaleteri* shops numbered 59.

Around 1493, these artisans adopted San Fantin for their patron saint— meaning they placed themselves and their pastries under his protection. They also founded a school of devotion at the church of San Fantin, opposite Teatro la Fenice on Campo San Fantin.

Not far from Rizzardini and near Campo San Polo, you'll find *Calle del Scaleter* (street of the pastry maker), a testimony to the time when many streets took their names from the craftsmen who lived and worked there.

At some point, the scalater became known as a *ciambellaio* after the term *ciambella*, another name for the special ladder-shaped cakes. Today in Venice, the *ciambella* is a small ring-shaped cake flavored with lemon zest or oranges, and the modern term for a pastry maker is *pasticciere*.

"Traditionally, the *pasticciere* came from the mountains," says owner Paolo Garlato, who took over Rizzardini in 1981 with the Pulese family, after selling glass on Murano for 20 years. "Those people developed the art of making *dolci* (sweets) and handed it down from father to son. After they made the *dolce*, others went down the mountain and sold them to shops and *osterie*," he continues.

The *pasticciere* at Rizzardini is Paolo Meggiato. "He has been with us for 20 years," says owner Paolo. "He's like the old-world pastry maker. *Appassionato* (passionate). He makes very good products. Everything we sell is made with the *ingredienti di prima scelta* (highest quality ingredients). If we pay less, we'll end up changing our products, which we won't do."

What's best to order at Rizzardini? Try one or more of these typical Venetian *dolci*: *ossi*, *amaretti*, *dogi*, *golosessi*, *marzapan*, *vini*, *pavana*, and *zaletti*. The latter has been around for a long time—Paolo can show you a *zaletti* recipe in a recipe book from the 1600s. During carnival, try the *frittelle*—very light, fried doughnuts, often flavored with raisins and lemon or orange peels. Pair any of the above with Paolo's excellent *caffé* (espresso), cappuccino, or *caffé macchiato* (*caffé* with a small stain of milk). He says, "Along with having good sweets, a pasticceria needs to have good *caffé*."

If you're not sure what to order, ask Paolo for a recommendation. He's happy to talk with you about pastries, the history of the city, Venetian glass—or just about anything. "I like the contact with the public. My job is to socialize and people come to find me. My wife, Anna, always says to me, 'You're wasting time. There's work to do.' This is part of my work… there are other things, too, of course. There's a lot to do in a small business like this," explains Paolo.

Rizzardini has its moods, which reflect the clientele. "In the morning, most people have to get to work. They drink a cappuccino or a *caffè* and take a *dolce* with them in a bag. They need to run," explains Paolo. "And then there are others not on a deadline, that have time. They drink a coffee and open the newspaper."

Late morning, you're likely to rub elbows with postal workers, judges and lawyers from the Tribunale, a professor or two from the local university, the president of the Venetian Hotel Owner's Association, and even Massimo Cacciari, off-and-on mayor of Venice since 1995. Cacciari graduated from the Università di Padova in philosophy and founded a number of philosophical and cultural journals. During his political career, he has tried to create a balance between the center right and center left parties.

Higher up the pecking order, there's member of parliament and high profile politico, Massimo D'Alema, who came in for a coffee a few years ago, and regular customers and "royals" Bianca di Savoia and her son, from the House of Savoy.

The Kingdom of Italy was formed in 1861 with the House of Savoy's Victor Emmanuel II at its head. He ruled until 1878, followed by son Umberto I. At this time the monarch lost much of his power and acted largely as a figurehead. Next in line, Victor Emmanuel III reigned from 1900 to 1946. Unpopular because of his association with Mussolini, he abdicated in favor of his son Umberto II. This attempt to save the monarchy failed: the Italian public voted for a republic in the 1946 referendum. The House of Savoy's rule ended, and Umberto's male heirs were banned from setting foot in Italian territory. In November 2002, this constitutional law was finally abolished.

In the afternoon, Rizzardini's mood changes once again. "Foreigners come to buy our specialties, and sometimes they stop to talk. I know a little of many languages, English, French, German. They ask questions, like 'Where can I find a good restaurant?' and 'How long will it take me to find a job here?'" says Paolo.

One of the first things you notice about Paolo are his piercing blue eyes, which seem to be a Venetian specialty, turning up indiscriminately on people such as the Carabinieri officer who's been taking tall, dark, and handsome lessons and the curvy Veneziana with the cascading, jet black curls.

A fourth-generation Venetian, Paolo has a boat parked in front of his Cannaregio house, instead of a car like the inhabitants of *terra ferma*. "I have a *topa*. It is a *barca tradizionale* (traditional boat), with a motor," says Paolo. "I take my wife out to catch some sun, visit the islands in the lagoon and fish, when the weather is nice." Originally designed to navigate the Venetian lagoon and nearby coastal waters under sail, the topa is now powered by an inboard motor. The name comes from *topo*, the Italian word for mouse. Viewed from underneath, the stern looks like the rear end of a mouse and the prow resembles its snout.

When he's not in the *pasticcieria* or on the water, Paolo likes to pass the time writing poetry. He's inspired by his city, by the sea, and, of course, by pastry. Paolo writes his poems in Veneziano, the Venetian dialect. Here is his "El Scaleter," translated into Italian:

Scaleter pasticciere
Non sono di famiglia.
Non sono di tradizione.
Ma lavoro in pasticceria
con tanta passione.

Da piccolo con una cesta in testa
correvo dove c'era una festa.

L'odore dei dolci si spandeva
per ponte, calle, campiei,

fino in salizada.
La gente si girava
e il naso tirava.

The following is an interpretation of Paolo's poem:

I am a *scaleter* (pastry maker).
I live only for my work,
for my passion.

As a child, with my head
a basketful of pastry dreams,
I ran to wherever there was a *festa*.

The perfume of fresh baked sweets
spilling into *calle*, *campo*, and *salizada*,
pulling everyone toward it.

Rizzardini has been here for a very long time—it offers the feel of old Venezia. It also offers some fantastic dolci *(sweets). Ask owner Paolo for some recommendations or just point. Either way, you can't go wrong. Coffee is good, and Paolo is chatty and full of life. This is an excellent spot to stop and regroup during your Venetian wanderings.*

· 5 ·

SANTA CROCE

Santa Croce has two faces: The charming "old Venice" section on the Grand Canal, where you can walk, usually, without running into hordes of tourists. And, there's the newer, utilitarian, and industrial part with Piazzale Michelangelo, the huge Tronchetto parking lot, and the Stazione Marittima—where you probably do not want to take your evening stroll. Santa Croce takes its name from a long gone church.

Alaska Gelateria-Sorbetteria

Calle Larga dei Bari
Santa Croce 1159
041 715211
Open daily noon–midnight,
May to September;
Noon–9PM, Tuesday to Sunday, October
to November and February to April
Closed December to January

The first time you make the journey to Alaska Gelateria you'll wander around Santa Croce for a lot longer than planned. The second time, however, you'll arrive in a fraction of the time. It's like that in Venice.

No matter, you'll always receive a genuine welcome from Alaska owner Carlo Pistacchi. He bought the place in 1988 and learned his gelato-making skills from the previous owner, some how-to books, and trial and error. "I try to follow the traditional methods and make gelato that is 100-percent natural. I modified the old recipes that I inherited because they were not all natural. Beware of gelato piled high in a mountain. It's not *gelato artigianale*. They pump lots of air into *gelato industriale* (industrial gelato) and it stands up high. The mountain is high; the quality is low."

Large ice cream manufacturers produce industrial gelato with high-tech equipment that aerates the end product so that it's very light—about 50 percent air, compared to about 15 percent with handmade artisan gelato. On a smaller scale, anyone can open a gelateria by simply renting a space; buying prepackaged base, syrup, and flavoring; and making industrial-style gelato. But the difference between this gelato and the handmade artisan product, where the base is made from fresh eggs, milk, and cream, is obvious once you do a taste test. The latter has a creamy texture and rich flavor from natural ingredients such as fresh strawberries, peaches, or melon—or real hazelnuts and dark chocolate.

"You don't get rich flavor from a package," says Carlo. All year round, he makes the classics—*cioccolato*, *nocciola*, *pistacchio*, and *mandorla*—but also branches out with unique seasonal tastes that are a little eccentric (like Carlo himself). In the spring, it's gelato flavored with small delicate carrots, fennel, and tiny white celery. Summer is the time for his light refreshing *sorbetto*, made with a water base and fresh fruit.

A vegetarian since 1986, Carlo personally consumes only produce that is *biologici* (organic), and only recently began eating meat and fish. To be certified

organic, a field in Italy has to be clean from chemicals or fertilizers for a minimum of 25 years. "In Sicily, right after World War II, many fields were purchased by Germans, who began organic farming in a way that made these fields free of chemicals by the 1950s," says Carlo. "These are truly organic fields and I have faith in them. Otherwise, lots of organic produce comes from fields that are not really purified. It takes a long time. And another thing, many of the aquifers are polluted, especially in the industrial north."

Oddly enough, there's a budding organic garden just behind the women's penitentiary on La Giudecca, the island shaped like a fish spine, just south of Venice. The penitentiary opened in 1859, in a 12th-century monastery, during the period of Austrian rule, and was put under the supervision of the Suore di Carità nuns. (Two-hundred-fifty years earlier, the very same monastery housed reformed prostitutes.) After the Austrian defeat in 1866, Venice, along with the Giudecca prison, returned to the newly minted Kingdom of Italy.

The initial goal for this enlightened facility was to rehabilitate through reeducation and meaningful work. Thus, it has continued to the present day, with daily activities that center around an organic garden, a workshop producing cosmetics, a tailor shop, and a laundry. Presently there are between 85 to 90 female inmates. Some are African and Asian, and about 40 to 45 percent have drug-addiction problems.

Carlo plans to give the prison's organic *orto* (market garden) a try. Called L'Orto delle Meraviglie (the garden of wonders), it covers about 4,000 square meters (43,056 square feet) of clean fields, free of industrial or agricultural contamination, and produces wonderful peppers, eggplant, tomatoes, potatoes, green onions, radicchio, artichokes, asparagus, and a variety of fruit, including blackberries, gooseberries, raspberries, and kiwi. It is managed by the Cooperativa Rio Terà dei Pensieri.

At the turn of the 19th century, Venetians had high hopes that La Giudecca would resuscitate the local economy as factories, including the abandoned (and highly visible) Mulino Stucky, were constructed along the inside of Canale della Giudecca facing Venice. This old flour mill's life span lasted from 1895 to 1954, much longer than that of owner, Swiss-born industrialist of Venetian origin, Giovanni Stucky. Although he pushed through the design for this monolith by threatening to fire all his 1,500 workers, and soon became one of the city's richest citizens, he enjoyed his success for only a short time. In 1910, a disgruntled employee killed him at the Venice train station. Stucky is probably smiling with approval from his grave at the completely restored Mulino Stucky, opened as a hotel and residential complex in June 2007.

There are two schools of thought about the origin of the name, La Giudecca. One claims that it was inhabited in early times by a community of Jews, who built two synagogues that were demolished in the last century. The other says the name came from the word *giudicato*, referring to a legal judgment in which the Barbalani, Flabanici, and Caloprini families were recalled from exile at the end of the 9th century and given land on La Giudecca as recompense for their pain and suffering.

Today, Carlo's neighborhood is known for his gelato, but a few centuries ago it was known for wool. Nearby sits Campo della Lana (little piazza of wool), home to a community of Germans famous for working with wool. The raw product arrived by the neighboring Rio Tolentini or Grande Canal and was cleaned and dyed.

From the 1500s until present, Venice has been known for producing the finest wool, silk, linen, cotton, velvet, satin, and brocade fabric. Two renowned textile producers still operate in Venice: Bevilacqua, founded in 1700, has workshops employing 100 people in the Santa Croce sestiere. The larger Rubelli, started in 1858, has its Venice design studio behind San Marco and a mill near Lake Como. With both firms, the quality is exceptionally high, as are the prices.

Roman-born Carlo has lived in Venice since he was 13. And in spite of his long residence there, he's still considered Romano. That's how it is in Italy—your city of birth defines you, even if you leave it when very young.

After high school, Carlo hit the road, working in France and England, and living for a year and a half on the streets in France. He describes it this way, "It was one of the most important experiences of my life. I was free 24 hours a day. I didn't have an objective or goal. I become aware that society is based on what people have to do. Everyone is after something and getting nowhere. But if you stop for a minute, there's time, and you can live slowly. I traveled around, hitchhiked. I went wherever the driver was going. I let myself be swept along by the current. I enjoyed this a lot because I found myself in beautiful places that I had no idea existed.

"During this time I didn't work. I lived with the minimum necessities. I slept in train stations," Carlo continues. "At that time in the early 1970s, everyone was more flexible. Now, there's rigidity, and that's understandable. The structure of the world has changed—everyone is afraid. And fear creates rigidity."

Carlo continues to make Venice his home because he likes to think, and the city's silent, moving canals create a soothing backdrop for his thoughts. Music is also an important part of his interior landscape—especially reggae, which he has collected since the early 1970s. "I have one of the best collections in the world from the period of '75 to '82, the golden age of reggae," Carlo says. "I have almost all the production that came from Jamaica. It's the main provider of reggae music worldwide, with a population of only six million people. The quantity of music that comes from the island is incredible. Reggae is my passion, more so than gelato."

Carlo has filled a 36-square-meter room and part of his cellar with his 25,000-record collection; most of it (15 to 20,000 records) is reggae. He believes strongly in reggae's message of promoting liberty, love, and peace.

His favorites include the genre's big three: Bob Marley (1945–1981), the prophet of reggae, best known for the hits *One Love*, *Three Little Birds*, and *No Woman*,

No Cry; Jimmy Cliff (b. 1948), famous for *Sittin' in Limbo*, *You Can Get It if You Really Want It*, and *The Harder They Come*; and Peter Tosh (1944–1987), who started with Bob Marley and the Wailers.

As for current reggae singers, Carlo says, "They're repetitive and less artistic. The exception being Luciano. He's both creative and he lives the message in his music." Originally from Manchester in the UK, Luciano shines as one of the brighter stars on the current reggae scene.

But it's not just reggae that interests Carlo. He finds ethnic music in general a direct form of communication, in the sense that if you don't understand lyrics in Masai, you can still understand the emotion in the music.

"I have a large map of the world. It's not so much a political map as a physical map, with rivers and mountains," says Carlo. "I've noticed the music of different places corresponds to the topography. The music of the desert is rarified and subtle. The music from areas by the water is very rhythmic. Music expresses the physicality of the world."

Carlo describes himself as *un po' bizzarro*; however, eccentric (and playful) is more like it. Here's an example: "I have some English friends who came to visit one summer and liked to play with water rifles," he says. "We had a huge battle in front of my gelateria. The following summer, during one hot day, I noticed my English friends approaching with their water rifles—I saw their refection in my shop windows. I didn't even know they were in Venice. So, quickly, I went in the bathroom to fill up my water rifle, and then lay down behind the *vetrina del gelato*. I knew they wouldn't be expecting this. I heard steps—someone entered. I was sure it was them.

"But it wasn't," continues Carlo. "It was one of my usual customers—a woman. I jumped up and shot her with water before I knew. She had big breasts and I soaked the front of her blouse. She yelled and I lost a client—even though I told her it was a mistake and a joke."

Another time, a Polish friend (an older woman) that he hadn't seen for years stopped by the gelateria. After visiting for a while, he escorted her to the nearby Santa Lucia train station. "When I'm gone from the store for a few minutes," says Carlo, "I always leave the door open." But this was for two hours. Walking back, he passed people eating his distinctive gelato, and he said to himself, "Carlo, what have you done! You're crazy. *Che confusione.* Everyone is helping themselves to the gelato."

Then, as he turned the corner to the gelateria, he saw an orderly line outside the door. There was a gentleman inside serving gelato, with his five-year-old boy collecting money. People made their own change. "I couldn't believe it," explains Carlo. "The man said he passed two or three times in front of the store, saw that no one was there, and decided to do something." Carlo had never met him before.

Yet another time, some kids came around to the gelateria selling used items, such as little newspapers and old toys, bundled in a sheet. Carlo says, "I like to buy things from kids, so I bought a small toy guitar with a microphone and an amplifier. Then I went around the street singing to the people: 'Come and eat my gelato.' Everyone laughed. Life is full of stress. My little joke helped discharge the tension."

This is vintage Carlo—he just wants to sell gelato, listen to reggae, and have fun.

Look for the messages scribbled on Alaska Gelateria's window—in many languages, including Japanese, Hebrew, Arabic, and Greek. The tradition started when a Japanese girl wanted to write nice things about Carlo's gelato. People often sign their names and sometimes are surprised to find something penned by a friend. While you're there, try Carlo's favorites: zenzero *(ginger) or* mandorla con arancia *(almond with lemon). You could brush elbows with the Mayor of Venice, Ziggy Marley, Inner Circle, or Emma Thompson. Carlo says the actress had a house nearby and, at one time, came here often.*

CAFÉ LISTINGS

Alaska Gelateria-Sorbetteria
Calle Larga dei Bari,
Santa Croce 1159
041 715211
Open daily noon–midnight, May to
September;
Noon–9PM, Tuesday to Sunday,
October to November & February to
April
Closed December to January

All'Arco
Calle de l'Ochialer,
San Polo 436
041 5205666
Open 8AM–5PM
Closed Sundays
Closed two weeks in August

Bar Aperol
Riva del Ferro,
San Marco 5125
O41 286304
Open daily 3AM–9PM

La Cantina
Strada Nuova, Campo San Felice
Cannaregio 3689
041 5228258
Open 10AM–10PM
Closed Sundays
*Closed two weeks July to August & two
weeks in January*

Cantinone "Già Schiavi"
Ponte San Trovaso
Dorsoduro 992
O41 5230034
Open 8:30AM–2:30PM, 3:30PM–8:30PM
Closed Sundays
Closed one week in August

Muro
Rialto San Polo 222
Venezia 30125
041 5237495
Open 9AM–3PM, 5PM–2AM
Closed Sundays

Osteria al Bacareto

Calle delle Botteghe
San Marco 3447
041 5289336
Open noon–3PM, 7PM–10:30PM,
Monday to Friday
Noon–3PM, Saturday
Closed Sundays
Closed August

Osteria al Diavolo e l'Aquasanta

Calle della Madonna
San Polo 561/B
041 2770307
Open 9:30AM–11PM, Wednesday to
Sunday
9:30AM–late afternoon, Monday
Closed Tuesdays

Osteria al Garanghelo

Calle dei Boteri
San Polo 1570-1571
O41 721721
Open Thursday–Tuesday,
10AM–8:30PM
*Closed Sunday evenings & Wednesdays,
and a few weeks in January & August
Closed Sundays & Wednesdays during
July and August*

Pasticceria Ballarin

Salizada San Giovanni Grisostomo
Cannaregio 5794
O41 5285273
Open daily 7:30AM–8PM

Pasticceria Didovich

Campo di Santa Marina 5908
San Marco
041 5230017
Open 7:30AM–8PM
Closed Sundays

Pasticceria Marchini

San Marco-Spaderia, 676
041 5229109
Open 8AM–5PM
Closed Sundays

Rizzardini

Campiello dei Meloni
San Polo 1415
O41 5223835
Open 7AM–9:30PM
Closed Tuesdays
Closed in August

Tonolo

Calle San Pantalon
Dorsoduro 3764
041 5237209
Open 7:45AM–8PM, Tuesday to
Saturday
7:45AM–1PM Sunday
Closed August

Torrefazione Caffé Costarica

Rio Terrà San Leonardo
Cannaregio 1337
O41 716371
Open 8AM–1PM, 2:30PM–5:30PM
Closed Sundays, except in December

Trattoria da Fiore

Calle delle Botteghe
San Marco 3461
041 5235310
Cichetteria open 9AM–11PM,
ristorante 12–3:30PM, 7–10:30PM
Closed Tuesdays
Closed from July 30–August 20

Alla Vedova

Ramo Ca' d'Oro
Cannaregio 3912
041 5285324
Open 11:30AM–2:30PM, 6:30–10:30PM,
Monday to Wednesday, Friday &
Saturday
6:30–11PM, Sunday
Closed Thursdays
Closed during August